INTERGOVERNMENTAL TRANSFERS: SOME ISSUES

INTERGOVERNMENTAL TRANSFERS

SOME ISSUES

P. DHIRAVIYAM

ABHIJEET PUBLICATIONS

DELHI 110094

ABHIJEET PUBLICATIONS
2/46 Tukhmeerpur Extension
Delhi-110 094
Phone: 011-22960492, 65698474
E-mail: abhijeetpublication@gmail.com

INTERGOVERNMENTAL TRANSFERS: SOME ISSUES

First Published 2008

ISBN 978-81-89886-98-1

PRINTED IN INDIA

Published by J.K. Singh for Abhijeet Publications, Delhi-110 094, Lasertypeset by Gaurav Graphics, New Delhi and Printed at Himanshu Printers, Delhi.

Dedicated

to

My Parents

A. PALANIAPPA PILLAI

& VAMBOYEAMMAL

Preface

Sharing of taxes and revenues between the central and state government is the most tedious job. There is an urgent need for settling revenue dispute between the two governments. In a federal setup like India the central Government is in a position to satisfy larger financial revenue exchequer. Financial sector in India has been underwent radical changes since 1991. The government has taken up various measures to improve the financial position from its backdrop. The government activated measurers like interest rate and monitory reforms to attract free inflow foreign capital and foreign direct investment. This book tries to bring out a real financial allocation between central and state government and also some emerging issues and other related settlement matters. Financial picture of our economy after the liberalization policy followed India. It also gives a clear cut picture of financial and monetary scenario.

To thank profusely scholars and authorities is a pleasure indeed.

I am greatly indebted to Dr. A. Arunachalam, M.A., M.Phil., M.L., Ph.D., M.B.A., Chairman and Correspondent of Adaikalamatha College, Vallam, Thanjavur.

I owe my sincere thanks to respected Principal Dr. R. KATHIAN, M.Com., M.Phil., Ph.D., for his timely help.

I owe my heartfelt thanks to T. Ravikumar, M.C.A. working as Software Engineer in Banglore for their constant encouragement. I feel happy to thank my father-in-law, mother-in-law, sister-in-law, brother-in-law and my wife Mrs. D. Santhi without their constant pressure and co-operation.

I will be failing in my duty if I could express my profound thanks to my daughters and sons for their timely help in bringing this book in time.

My profound thanks to beloved sisters and brothers who's put me in the right and pious path in my life.

I owe my sincere thanks to Co-operative Manager, Canara Bank Manager for their moral and financial support to undertake this research.

I am thankful to Abhijeet Publications, New Delhi for their Interest and co-operation in publishing this book.

I do not claim that could cover all the aspects of the financial scenario of India under globalisation within the limited space, but I firmly believe that this book will be very useful to all concerned.

P. DHIRAVIYAM

May 2008

THANJAVUR

Contents

1

Economic Criteria for Intergovernmental Transfers: Some Issues

Introduction

The design of intergovernmental transfers is an important issue in federal countries not only because the sub-national governments often depend on these to maintain their supply of public services, but also because the various elements of the determination of transfers may have incentive effects for the sub-national governments. These may not be taken into account fully while designing the transfers and may thus have unintended effects.

The reasons for intergovernmental grants are similar across nations, although the actual applicability of and emphasis on each of these reasons may very with the way public finance are organized in particulars cases. As several reviews of intergovernmental transfers point out, there are six basic reasons ameliorating vertical imbalance, reducing horizontal imbalance correcting for inter-jurisdictional spillovers ensuring minimum standards of basic-services paying for agency functions undertaken by sub-national governments and returning revenues to lower level governments as a part of a tax-rental arrangement. Clearly an evalution of a transfer's system—or an element thereof—requires an understanding of the objectives involved and an assessment of the extent to which the objective is met. Additionally there are some desirable features that the transfers system should have mainly arising from efficiency considerations, but also to ensure that the system meets the relevant objectives in practice. These include adequacy regularity transparency and feasibility, it is possible to add to these. An overarching consideration is that of the incentives built into the system. The safest system from this point of view would be one that based transfers on variables completely outside the control of the recipient governments.

In this paper, we examine the transfer system that operates in India through the institution of the finance commission (which implies that plan transfers and discretionary transfers are excluded from its scope). The focus is on an evalution of the need appropriateness and manner of use of various socio-economic criteria in the design of transfers mandated by finance.

Use Indicators at all

To start a discussion of the indicators used in the Indian intergovernmental transfer schemes, one must begin with the need for formula-based transfers that necessitate the use of the indicators. After all, not every nation with multi-tier governmental structure use them. One alternative that we are inclined to dismiss summarily is a system comprising solely of discretionary of bargain-based transfers. While such transfers do exist in some countries including India, they are never the only type of transfer nor are they good in that they severely affect the autonomy of the states, are uncertain and actually an appropriate one in court view, would be a system based completely on normative assessments of revenue and expenditures, with transfers filling up the normative deficits. In case transferable is the system used in Australia.

The reasons for our preference for such a system, of course. Are that it combines equity consideration with these of efficiency in the best possible manner. The critics of the gap-filling approach used in India earlier have discusses this issue at great length, which need not be repeated. In fact probably in response to these criticisms, the terms of reference for the ninth finance commission explicitly advocated a normative approach for the distribution of deficit grants an attempt was duly made to use this approach but in the end, the bottom lines were not really affected very much by the approach because: *(a)* formula-based tax devolution as a first step took a large number of states out of the ambit of deficit grants, *(b)* the normative estimates were diluted ostensibly to make the transition easier, and *(c)* substantial grants for special purpose ruined any objectivity that the system might have had. It also clearly lacked transparency as the critical chorus of state government official about not under standing the system during the working of the commission and immediately after the report was submitted, showed. Arguably the understanding of the normative approach has improved since then.

It should be noted here that the use normative approach does not rule out the use of indicators altogether, but only the direct use in computing amounts of transfers. For example, normative assessment, of say health expenditures in various states can be done on the basis of an econometric exercise using a number of health status indicators and indicators of cost disabilities but this example also serves to illustrate why complete reliance on the normative approach has not found widespread favour in India. The data requirements for such an approach is large, as respectable normative assessments can only be done in a disaggregated framework. It also requires quite a bit of work, which in turn requires more time for the finance commission to complete its job than they normally have in fact a permanent institution like the commonwealth grants commission is the logical complement of a system based completely on normative assessments.

How does one rationalize a transfer system based on indicators then? For us distribution formula using such indicators would be only an approximation of a full-blown normative assessment, perhaps with a greater degree of transparency. To put it in another way, a formula based on socio-economic indicators may be interpreted as the reduced form of a set of structural equations. If normative expenditure in state I (E) is a function of a set of variables X just as revenue capacity (R1) is a function of a similar set of variables Y and the two sets of variables X and Y are determined by a single set of exogenous variables Z (the second subscript is different to indicate that the number of determinants need not be the same as for either expenditures or revenue) then it can be seen that the difference between normative revenue and expenders can be expressed as a function of Z. This third set of exogenous variables may or may not contain variables from X and Y. Then transfers based on normative deficits should be linked to Z in the reduced from. When K is small and the variables are easy to understand, a formula driven transfer system will be both efficient and transparent.

Vertical and Horizontal Imbalance

The first issue relating to imbalances that needs reflection is that of considering the objectives of vertical and horizontal balance separately. It is possible to argue that in the context of individual states, both are reflected in a single indicator, the normative deficit. In such a case, if the distribution formula is implicitly based on normative deficit, then why should one bother to consider them separately? In fact transfer system such as the Australian one do not and are probably correct in doing so. But as we shall see below this is not necessarily true of all formula-driven transfer that may be implicitly based on normative deficits.

A formula driven system of transfer even when implicitly based on normative deficits does not necessarily cover the inter normative deficit are not known in such a system, precisely because they are not known that an approximating formula is required. It follows that if a relatively better-off-state, which may only have a small imbalance is overcompensated, it would mean that state is getting more than what it should get to cover its share of vertical imbalance while it should not be entitled to any transfer based on horizontal imbalance at all. There would then necessarily be some other state that would get less than its due unless the total distribution kitty is larger than what it ought to be in the latter case the system would be inefficient as it would use up more funds than strictly required and would be particularly inappropriate when the grantor government is itself in deficit. The seriousness of this problem varies with the way the formula is applied. The system can conceptually provide for both positive and negative grants for individual states. Germany is one example of such a system, but it is in fact rare. In such a system, the problem of overcompensation would not exist, and the negative transfers would be fully attributable to equalization, i.e., promoting horizontal equity. Another system would be of positive transfers up to a point (the norm) and states above that level receive zero transfer. The Canadian system, and the Indian system of deficit grants would be examples of this. Even here the overcompensation problem is not present unless there are other elements of the transfer system that cause the outcome to be different (as in India). The problem would however be solved if all states necessarily received positive amounts, as in the case of tax sharing in India, quantitatively far more significant than deficits.

Vertical imbalance is by definition a concept that is applicable to a particular level os sub-national units as a whole and allocating the overall imbalance among individual units is not conceptually easy. When the transfer system has to be designed on the basis of available information on budgetary outcomes that mix up vertical and horizontal imbalance (and possibly some amount of fiscal sloth and/or inefficiency). Perhaps the best way of conceptually separating them normative deficit of the state with the smallest such deficit, for each of the sub-national units [Bird and Smart 2002]. After taking care of the vertical imbalance in this fashion the remaining deficits can then be ascribed to horizontal imbalance and dealt with in an appropriate manner. Thus any system that has an element of a small amount of equal transfer for all recipient units, normalized for the size of the individual units, could be said to have dealt with vertical imbalance, at least approximately clearly one does not need any indicator or formula for achieving this a rough idea of the smallest normative deficit would be enough.

If normative deficit are not being assessed and covered then it is equalization where the role of a formula and indicators becomes important. This is actually the case in several federal systems, where the explicit objective of using a formula is equalization (e.g., Canada, Germany UK, Nigeria and South Africa). India is an odd case where normative assessments are made and used for one type of transfers, but without any explicit articulation of the objective (except in recent reports of FCs). An equalization type formula is being used for another (fiscally more significant) type of transfers as well it must be pointed out that the appropriateness of a formula or the constituent criteria thereof depends heavily on the type of transfer instrument and the objectives sought to be achieved.

Evolution of the Indian Transfer System

The ambivalence characterizing the Indian system is noticeable from the way the relevant constitutional provisions and the distribution formula have evolved over the years. We briefly summaries this process in this section and then proceed to a discussion of the various criteria in the next.

The statutory transfers in India consisted of three different parts to begin with income tax sharing, excise duty sharing and the grants-in-aid while the grants are clearly meant enhancement of fiscal capacity, the constitutions does not spell out the objectives of tax sharing. The three way transfer system follows faithfully the relevant constitutional provisions, and different (sets of) criteria were used to distribute transfers through these three channels. Until the Eighth Finance Commission (hereafter FC) brought on other criteria, the sharing of income tax was only on the basis of the neutral criterion of population. With a much smaller weight given to derivation. The first and second FCS distributed the share of union excise duties simply on the basis of population but the latter kept aside 10 per cent for discretionary allocation. The 3rd FC added financial weakness and economic backwardness to the major factor of population introducing an element of equalization into tax sharing but the weights were not specified. The 4th used the same factors with 80 per cent and 20 per cent weights respectively. The 5th 6th and 7th FCs further added per capita income as a distribution criterion for excise duties. The 6th FC dropping the backwardness factor. The 7th FC used an explicit revenue equalization criterion in the distribution of excise duties.

There were a number of breaks from tradition in the recommendations of the 8th FC. For the first time an element of equalization was brought into the distribution of income tax too with the use of per capita income in two different forms (discussed in some detail in the next section). Also for the first time, a part of the shareable excise duties was set aside exclusively for the deficit states, a feature continued until the 11th FC. The general distribution formula contained the population criterion along with two forms of the income criterion. The 9th FC, in its two reports, added the criterion of poverty and index of backwardness alternately to the variables included by the 8th in the distribution of the states share of income tax, and the union excise duty.

The awards of the 10th FC again were characterized by departures from the trend. It completely dropped the derivation criterion for the first time. It also used the same distribution formula for the states shares of both income tax and excise duty, a step recommended by researchers for some time but not very popular in certain quarters because of the market emphasis on equalization. The formula included the criteria of area, index of infrastructure and tax effort for the first time, besides the more orthodox criteria of population and (some variant of) per capita income. Finally it recommended an alternative scheme of tax sharing with a fixed share of all union tax revenues to be set aside for distribution to states on the basis of a single formula. This recommendation was accepted with some modifications in the definition of the distributable pool. And necessary constitutional amendment was carried out. The 11th FC gave its recommendations under the new system, essentially continuing with the same criteria as used by the 10th, with one minor change. Fiscal discipline was substituted for tax effort.

Grants-in-aid have been distributed on the basis of projected deficits remaining after the tax devolution. As the successive FCs widened the coverage of tax sharing, the relative size of shared taxes rose in comparison to grants, until grants, became almost insignificant in the awards of the 10th FC. The 11th FC reversed this to some extent. But the overall trend towards greater reliance on tax devolution compared to grants, along with progressively stronger emphasis on equalization in the devolution of taxes is unmistakable.

Criteria for Distribution

For an assessment of various criteria that have been in use by the successive FCs in India, and similar criteria used elsewhere, perhaps the best way is to group similar one commonly in use and other criteria by the objectives sought to be achieved. This has the advantage of facilitating a discussion of pros and of similar criteria together and allowing us to take a view on the best alternative. But before we start the discussion on the various criteria, it may be appropriate, in view of the importance of the transfers in the sub-national budgets, to lay down a few features that ideally characterize the information base base/variables used should:

- Be statistically sound complied using common principles.
- Be available and comparable across units of governments.
- Be as up-to-date as possible and regularly reviewed.
- Come from an independent source to the extent possible so that the different levels of government cannot manipulate them.
- Be different in effect from other variables, and
- Reflect needs or demands for public goods (for example the number of clients), instead of physical input measures.

Equalizing Fiscal Capacity: Income–Based Criteria

Variants of the income criterion have been in used in India since the 5th FC. There are other federations (e.g., Brazil and China) that use this criterion for intergovernmental transfers, but several developing countries lack the necessary data to make use of it. In general, this criterion appears to be directly linked to interstate equity, and therefore ought to be a progressive and redistribute one, ideal for equalization. But the limitations imposed by available data, under a priori standing and ambiguities about the best from of this variable to be used have marred its utllity despite its consistent use by the last seven FCs (and incidentally, the Planning Commission).

Ideally, the income variable to be used, if at all, is the personal disposable income, or the state level counterpart of the per capita national income. Unfortunately, this is not available and gross/net domestic product is used instead. The problem with this is that neither the productive capacity of the state nor the purchasing power in the hand of the residents is accurately reflected in the estimated figures. The problems relating to actual location of the productive activity (Doglike 2003) and to large amounts of remittances are well known.

The case for including an income variable with a negative association is usually predicated upon a positive link of income with fiscal capacity and not regional inequality per sent? While it is true that lower incomes can reasonably be expected to lower revenue capacity, it is also true that most researchers find positive link between demand for public goods and income as well. Then the net increase in fiscal capacity with rising incomes becomes uncertain and so does the utility of income as a retention in a distribution formula. International experience reveals that relatively few developing countries explicitly attempt to assess sub-national fiscal capacity due to their lack of detailed data on revenue bases. Direct capacity measures are more common in transfer formulas of developed countries, as is the case in Japan, Australia or Canada. It is therefore quite is proxies with the help of a Marco index such as the GSDP in India. But this rough approximation is precarious, as it is doubtful whether the GSDP properly represents a states revenue raising capacity. Also GSDP data could conceivably by subject to manipulation (the so-called comparable estimates are after all based on state level data with some marginal adjustments). Resulting in bad intergovernmental comparability. Given its overwhelming importance in the allocation formula, one should certainly keep in mind the considerable impact of even small inexactitudes in the measurement of GSDP and its general inappropriateness to represent a states ability to pay. The inclusion of such a fiscal capacity proxy in the allocation formula could potentially do more harm than good, particularly in combination with large weights.

Two variants of the income criterion have been used in India, for some time in tandem, the distance criterion and the inverse income criterion. The distance criterion reflects disparities in the states per capita income and measures their absolute relative disparities. The implications of using these alternative formulations differ, middle income states lose out with the latter as compared to the former. Using the two together (with the same total weight) should put the distribution between those implied by either of them. With the relative weights determining the exact location. There have been other adjustments made in the use of this indicator e.g. in the definition of the highest income. The sum total of all this fine tuning is to equity at least in the interest of simplicity, a straightforward distance formula should be used. And given the problems associated with this criterion, a lower weight should be attached to it, even if it implies an apparently less progressive distribution. After all the moral hazard relating to rewarding lower growth also needs to be taken into account further if this is taken as a proxy for fiscal capacity, then serves consideration should given to computing and using the same directly.

Evening Out Different Levels of Expenditure Needs

The population criterion: the population criterion reflects the assumption that a states expenditure needs generally grow proportionally with the number of its inhabitants. Although it is not a progressive criterion by itself, it has considerable equalizing impact the criterion does not take into account the differences of states in their fiscal capacities, but provides equal per capita transfers to all states.

Population is an important and commonly used allocation factor in transfer formula around the world. In fact population based revenue sharing has clear advantages, it is a simple and transferring indicator, rather objective and provides a high degree of predictability several countries around the globe, like Brazil, Pakistan, Colombia, Germany, Spain, Portugal and Italy, rely heavily on the population variable for the distribution of general purpose grants.

We believe that population in principle is an appropriate and objective allocation factor as it targets every citizen as the ultimate client of public services—equally however it is elementary to ensure that accurate and timely data are used in the distribution formula. Unfortunately this is not the case for the FC allocation formula in India. The finance commission is politically bound to use census data of 1971 for the calculation of the population-based shares. Even though census information on 1981, 1991 and 2001 is available. The objective in using the 1971 population front. This provision is bad in law (there, are no constitutional provisions in this regard), bad in theory (states are penalized for in-migration, for reduction in mortality rate and because they are poorer) and bad in practice (in relative terms, the maximum loss is to the special category states) [Srivastava and Seen 2000].

Apart from these serious data flaws, one can point out that the small weight acceded to population does not correspond to its strong influence on expenditure needs. There seems to be no theoretically plausible reason, why successive FCs have consistently the weight of population in the allocation formula. Given its current low weight and due to the inappropriate usage in the FC formula, we feel that the population variable is not used as it could be ideally and has lost much of its initial appeal. It is true that it is implicitly used in the various FC formula whenever any variable is defined in per capita terms, but in practically all such cases, its use is essentially as a normalizing factor, which is quite different from use of population per se as a variable in its own right.

The area criterion: the area indicator is intended to reflect cost disadvantages to state governments for providing basic services to its citizens. Less densely populated area typically require higher levels of government services and these create higher costs [Martinez-Vazuez and Boex 2002]. A good example of such cost disabilities would be the desert areas in

Rajasthan where small village a situated at large distances from each other raise the per capita costs of providing basic services as well as infrastructure. Because of this, many other countries such as Indonesia, Italy, Nigeria, Brazil and Philippines have explicitly incorporated the criterion of geographical size in their allocation formula.

But the other side of the coin, with respect to the use of area (or population density) is that the costs of delivering public services tend to be higher in very densely populated areas as well the well known Bumbles cost-disease hypothesis. In fact in Germany city-states receive higher allocation due to the advantage of urbanization. Similar arrangements can be found in Korea and again Japan [Bird and Treason 2002, Alms and Martinez-vazquez 2002]. On the local level, in France even an urban solidarity compensation was established supporting municipalities with more than 10,000 inhabitants [PWC 2000]. To be sure this consideration applies more to the cities than states, but it could be relevant for highly urbanized states or states with a number of congested cities too. Since a part of the burden of the local government tends to get transferred to the state government in the Indian context of limited flexibility of local governments to meet these special requirements.

Sometimes, other special vocational characteristics are also in the reckoning the Swiss grant formula used to include a factor that recognizes increased costs for cantons in mountainous area [Teflon 1999] and in Nepal there have been lengthy discussions about including a remoteness variable in the formula design [Boex 2002]. Similarly in the South African grant formula each rural person is counted as equal to 1.25 urban persons in recognition of the special problems of the rural areas [Ahmad 1998]. Countries like Morocco or Colombia categories their localities even more accurately according to their size by type and sometimes by region. Such attempts have sometimes proved to be helpful guides to general expenditure needs [Bird and Smart 2002]. To adjust the standard unit cost of providing public services in disadvantage regions, Japan uses several modification coefficients such as cold climate or rapid population decrease [Alm and Martine-Vazuez 2002]. In Malawi, 13 per cent of grants are distributed on per capita basis exclusively to a number of drought–stricken regions [Martinez-Vazuez and Boxe 2002]. Thus there is plenty of support on the use of geographical characteristics in general in the formula for distributing transfers.

While introducing the area for the first time, the 10th FC itself highlights some of the weaknesses of the area indicator their report recognizes that costs do not necessarily increase proportionately with the size of the states. There are economies of scale to be considered also, and states with very small areas or with hilly terrain would face higher than proportionate per capita costs. To allow for these deficiencies and to avoid excessive variations in resource allocations among state governments on this count they established an upper and lower end to the area based overall share of the states. The 11th Finance Commission has adopted these floor and ceiling limits of 2 per cent 20 per cent whereas the weight of the indicator has been augmented without any clear justification. In any case it should be pointed out that indicators such as population density or territorial size are very rough proxies of actual expenditure needs and are therefore always somehow unsatisfactory, but they do have the advantage of avoiding the moral hazard problem, being outside the control of the state governments. However it needs to be kept in mind that ultimately all the factors considered above are indirect ways of approximating differences in cost of public service provision, if some way can be found to do it directly that would obviate the need for these proxies and would clearly be a better method.

Poverty and backwardness criteria: the 9th FC poverty as a criterion in its first report despite recognizing the serious data and methodological problems involved but better sense prevailed at the time of the submission of the final report. While removal of poverty is undoubtedly a laudable general objective, it is harpy the right one for a transfer formula nor is it a good indicator of expender need. First it is much better targeted though specific purpose transfers (with or without matching requirements), as it is being done in India. Second at the time it was used poverty was not even a good indicator of either revenue capacity or cost disability, the example of Maharashtra (that had high per capita income as also relatively high levels of poverty) would suffice to make this point. Finally it is an outcome that is not outside the control of the states public policy has a lot to do with the incidence of poverty. In this situation using poverty estimates for distributing transfers could easily provide the wrong incentives.

In comparison, the backwardness criterion used by the second report of the 9th FC does not suffer from these problems. It can perhaps be improved by rationalizing and widening the variable as the percentage of population dependent on government expenditure (besides the scheduled caste and the scheduled tribe population, it could include children of school-going age, senior citizens, the disabled and other such categories), but it certainly has advantage of not being influenced by government policy except in the very long run.

The infrastructure criterion; the introduction of the infrastructure criterion by the 10th FC in 1995 was meant to compensate state governments with smaller infrastructure endowments. It can be interpreted as a criterion that reflects cost deficiencies of a state. The assumption involved is that the greater the infrastructure deficiencies of a state are the greater will be its costs of providing public services [Srivastava 2003].

However the finance commission explicit reason for incorporating the infrastructure criterion has been to promote development and growth of backward states. The ultimate aim is to improve living conditions, educational services and investment appeal of disabled regions [Report of the 10th Finance Commission, p. 176]. This desire is of course understandable though in this context of unconditional general-purpose grants it is not at all convincing. If the center wishes to foster the development of infrastructure in disadvantaged and poorer regions it should rather consider conditional specific-purpose grants, which are targeted and can be properly regulated.

The FC infrastructure index of the states is a weighted combination of economic and social infrastructure indices, which in turn are composed of a number of sub-indices. The economic infrastructure index consists of data on agriculture, banking electricity, transport and communication facilities. The social infrastructure indicator contains data on educational and health service endowments, such as the number of hospital beds or primary schools. The weight of the infrastructure criterion has been raised to 7.5 per cent by the 11th FC, with no clear justification in their report.

It is generally considers a bad practice in grant design to include the level of infrastructure availability as an allocation factor [Martinez-vazquez and Boex 2002]. Notwithstanding this negative assessment, some countries other than index have used criteria based on physical infrastructure measures. Examples would be Nigeria and Ethiopia. Argentina in the 1970s had a transfer formula which included an index of the development gap based on measures of housing quality the number of vehicles and the educational level [Bird and Vaillancourt 1998].

Using an infrastructure index in the transfer formula fails several tests of a good indicator of cost disability. Its use can provide the wrong incentives, since it is not exogenous to the system, the recipient governments play a major role in the provision of infrastructure. Since the states with lesser infrastructure attain higher transfers, the index clearly provides incentives to the states not to invest in the creation and maintenance of infrastructure, as this measure would indirectly decrease future grant transfers. This index is based on inputs and outcomes. Whereas an index of need would be the right one to use. The needs of a state could be easily quantified by the number of potential clients that should receive respective services or transfers (e.g., the number of school-aged children and elderly people).. The grant literature widely agrees on this general rule for the assessment of sub-national needs [Martinez-vazquez and Boex 2002], Bird and Vaillancourt 1998] and rejects input-based variables such as the FC infrastructure index.

In the Indian context, there is another aspect that

needs to be noted. While the use of infrastructure index may reward states with how value explicitly this is substantially undone in the computation of deficit grants. The assessed expenditure needs usually take the existing stock of infrastructure and allow for maintenance on such stock. This method results in lower maintenance costs allowed for states with poor infrastructure can, calling out the gains through the explicit use in the distribution formula. At the present juncture there are further complications with the use of this variable, due to an enhanced role of the private sector in the provision of infrastructure the objective of promoting reforms may dictate unambiguous rewards for enhanced availability of infrastructure but the fact remains that to the extent it is privately financed government resources do not have to be augmented through transfers. Overall the various problems relating to the use of infrastructure index suggest that it is a variable better not used in the transfer formula, instead, a variable that more directly approaches the issue by defining potential clients or the need for infrastructure should be used to steer clear of the moral hazard problem.

Fiscal Performance Criterion: Bringing About Budgetary Balance

The fiscal performance criterion embedded in the FC devolution formula aim to correct possible systemic disincentives and foster fiscal discipline of state governments. Redistribution and voluminous intergovernmental transfers per se are said to have discouraging effects both on revenue raising [Lalvani 2002] and expenditure restraints of the states. While the worries about proper incentive compatibility and sub-national fiscal prudence are surely justified there are some serious problems and policy concerns about the integration of various fiscal performance criterion in a redistribute grant system. The basis criterion has taken two different forms so far as the devolution formulae are concerned, but other forms have been used by the FC in deciding debt relief.

Tax Effort Criterion: The tax effort criterion introduced by the 10th FC and continued by the 11th aims to reward the states' revenue performance. A state receives a higher share in the FC tax devolution the more it exploits its presumed tax base. Due to the alleged lack of suitable data on the diverse sub national tax bases, he commission uses the GSDP as a proxy for the states taxable capacity. Tax effort is therewith defined as the ratio of per capita own tax revenue of a state to its per capita GSDP. This simple tax GSDP ratio is then additionally weighted with the inverse of the states' GSDP, to take into account revenue raising disabilities of poorer states. Apart from the fact that GSDP is a very simplistic indicator and does not take into account a large number of factors directly influencing the raising capacity of a state, and that better estimates of tax effort can certainly be made, there are a priori reasons for not considering tax effort good distributive criterion.

As McLure (1997) argues: It is difficult to justly including tax effort in grant formulas. It runs counter to the purpose of fiscal decentralization, which is to allow sub-national governments to decide how much tax effort to put forth. In fact the degree of tax exploitation ultimately depends on the political and ideological determination of each state government. State have different expenditure philosophies and a state should not receive additional equalization transfers as a reward for levying more taxes of provide an above average standard of public services. This criterion may be suitable for a highly centralized system where sub national governments have no autonomy with respect to determining tax rate or base and are expected to administer the tax laws as best as they can. India is clearly not such federation. It is an imperfect indicator of fiscal efficiency too, simply because it is one-sided and does not take into account the expenditure side of the budget. In a situation of widespread deficits, the anxiety to encourage tax effort and reduce the deficits in under standable; but the inherent problems associated with this criterion suggest that it should be used sparingly only when there is reason to believe that the state in general are lacking in tax effort. There is broad agreement on the theoretical prescription that in the long run, federal policies should try to neither discourage nor encourage tax efforts, and should be neutral.

Rewarding regions that exert higher levels of fiscal effort does not support the optimal distribution and allocation of public expenditures. Instead it might result in the use of federal resources on inappropriate or even wasteful local projects. To highlight the perverse outcome of the introduction of a tax effort criterion (like the one applied by the FC) imagine a state which has been successful in attracting investment and new economic activities due to the efficient provision of public services and low taxes. This state will be penalized twofold at the time of great allocation. Both its supposedly low tax effort and the increased GSDP will lower the states position in the FC tax effort index resulting in lower transfers.

There are a number of countries that attempt to

include explicit measures of fiscal effort in their distributive formulae. These include Colombia, Korea, Nigeria, Pakistan, Romania and Spain. Critical assessments of some of these systems generally indicate no impact on fiscal effort, and worse, significant allocative distortions (Ahmad and Baer 1997: Shan 1998: Martinez-Vazquez 2002; Romanik et al 1999). In the Indian context, additional difficulties with the tax effort index relate to its distortion through tax exportation by more developed states and possible non-linearities in the relation between the tax base and the tax revenue.

To sum up, it is likely that high price is paid to motivate the states to rise higher taxes, which may not come about in practice, and may not even be desirable. The 11th FC lowered the weight of the tax effort criterion to 5 percent, but introduced the fiscal discipline criterion that has its own problems.

Fiscal discipline criterion: Essentially drive by the rising sub national current and fiscal deficits, the 11th Finance Commission for the first time incorporate a fiscal discipline variable in the devolution normal. The FC actually constructed an index of fiscal improvement, which compares the ratio of a state's own revenue receipts to its total revenue expenditure with a similar ratio for all states . The idea is to reward states that have done relatively better in terms of their revenue balance. The better the performance of state in achieving revenue balance relative to others, the higher its share in devolution. (Srivastava 2003). It is a performance criterion, which measures relative fiscal improvements in a reference period compared to a specific bas e period. Given the serious fiscal concerns in India, this innovative variable might appear appropriate on first sight, but a careful analysis shows serious weaknesses.

First of all, defining the criterion in terms of the change over a base year value can create a problem of rewarding past sins. It is generally through to be easier to improve upon bad performance as against good. Further the average against which a particular state 's performance is judged is also in terms of change. Hence, when very state is doing badly a state that only maintains it base year performance—good or bad— is rewarded. Thus, the encouragement to achieve fiscal discipline may not be string. While these criticisms are correct in general, the use of the criterion has to be judged in the particular context of widespread deficits and more as a fire fighting measure than as a standard or regular one. Also, the use of levels instead of change is debatable in that it would perpetuate the fiscal advantages of the better-off states. Moreover, it is not quite clear, in the context of Indian state finances, whether it is really easier to improve upon low values than higher values of the performance indicator. Much of the revenue deficits consist of interest payments in the case of almost all states, and large deficits tend to cause increased borrowing resulting in higher interest payments and higher future deficits. This vicious circle is weaker for states with low deficits ad relatively easy to break out of, as compared to high-deficit states. It is therefore not the technical flaws, but the conceptual problems that we think are the clinching arguments.

First, this type of incentive for achieving a revenue balance cannot distinguish between different ways of achieving the improvement in fiscal discipline. Reduction in expenditures and increasing revenues are both possible routes to improve the balance. And this can be done through raising distortionary taxes and/or reducing good expenditures. The effect of this criterion on the efficiency of the use of public resources is really unpredictable. Second, it fails to distinguish between spendthrift governments and those having deteriorating revenues balance due to factors beyond their control, e.g. natural calamities, economic downturn originating form macroeconomic factors, law ad order problems or social unrest. Third, there is political economy angle that may be considered a weakness of this criterion. In the federal setup of India, such a requirement may impinge on the fiscal autonomy of the states, and is not justifiable unless there are clear spillovers of their fiscal policies. Even when there are negative spillovers, unless the grantor government itself exhibits fiscal prudence, the case for liking fiscal discipline with distribution of constitutionally ordinal transfers may not be convincing.

But probably the greatest flaw of this criterion is that it is unlikely to have substantial incentive effect at all. Taking into account the entire political and federal fiscal framework, there is no great incentive for a short-term elected government to behave in a fiscally prudent manner. A government faces the trade-off between raising more debt (and speculating on federal gap filling) and being fiscally disciplined to receive the reward of higher FC tax devolution. The future increases of FC tax devolutions due to fiscal prudence will however probably be much smaller than the volume attainable through debt. A state government facing strong political pressure on a daily basis is therefore more likely to continue on the easy path of high deficit than to fight for rather uncertain future FC rewards. As long as the center cannot establish and keep up any efficient hard budget constraints, the fiscal discipline criterion will not prevent imprudent fiscal stances and increasing debt burden.

Collection/Assessment Criterion: Returning Tax Revenues to Originating Jurisdictions

This criterion was in the from the very first FC to the 9th, after which it was discontinued by the 10th, and has so far not reappeared. The weight attached to it varied between 10 and 20 percent. While its removal has made the overall formula more equitable, it has predictably been criticized by the restively developed states. In theory, the origin criterion is appropriate for the distribution of the proceeds of a tax when it is presumed to be ideally in the domain of the states, but for some reason (usually administrative, but in the interest of uniformity too) is levied and collected by the center. The idea in such a case is to approximate the revenues that a state would have collected had it administered the tax itself.

Going by this logic, use of this criterion can possibly be justified for the additional excise duties (on sugar, textiles ad tobacco, the power to levy sales tax on which was surrendered by the states to the center through a tax rental agreement) and the taxes that the states could have collected if the Centre did not abolish them (e.g. tax on railway passengers) or did not ignore them (taxes listed under Article 269 of the Constitution). Except for the last category, net proceeds (hypothetical after abolition) from the other taxes were actually distributed on the origin basis until the alternative scheme of devolution was implemented. But the use of this criterion for the distribution of income tax was not supported by this logic, as there has never been a presumption in India that non-agricultural income tax was also ideally included in the domain of the states. In fact, the record of the states in taxing agricultural income, a power that was assigned to them by the Constitution is dismal. Most states do not use this power at all, and those that do, confine is application to plantations only, creating loopholes that can be exploited in evading non agricultural income tax.

At present, since the entire tax revenue of the Centre is shareable en bloc, there is possibly case for the use of this criterion with a very small weight , to compensate for the fact that the amounts that used to be (with justification) distributed on the basis of origin have been submerged in the aggregate.

Conclusion

In the Indian system of statutory transfers, criteria-based transfers apply to tax sharing only. The deficit grants are given on the basis of post-devolution assessed deficits alone. While there may be several observations that one can make on the process of estimating these deficits, this is beyond the scope of this paper. Of course, it is difficult to assess any element of a transfer system in isolation, since these elements usually complement each other. This is particularly true of the objectives of the transfer system, the tools used and the process of distribution.

We have argued that if the primary concerns of our transfer system are to eliminate vertical imbalances and enable the states to minimize horizontal imbalances, then it is necessary to conceptually sèparate them out. Since it is possible to think of vertical imbalance as the minimum deficit among the individual states generalized to all states, a small amount of transfer for each state, suitably scaled up or down for the size, perhaps with population, should be adequate. This would leave the more difficult question of equalizing fiscal capacity without building in the wrong incentives. While maintaining certain other virtues like simplicity, predictability and regularity. Unfortunately, experience shows that there is a trade-off between conceptually the best system of equalization, that of a full–blown normative assessment and simplicity. In such a situation, various criteria are used to implement a formula based system as an approximation. Moreover, if tax shares were small and the grants constituted the primary channel of center-state transfers, then it would be possible to dispense with a complex distribution formula. The tax sharing would cover vertical imbalance and the grants distributed on the basis of normative deficits, as is done now, would take care of equalization. But in fact shared taxes are much large than required to meet vertical imbalance alone, and from this fact arises the need to use distribution formulate that include factors representing fiscal equalization.

To maintain the basic features of the normative assessment system, revenue capacity and expenditure needs have to be reflected in the formula used. Not all transfer systems use the two-pronged approach, however. While some equalize revenue capacity only (e.g. Canada), other only look at expenditure needs (e.g. South Africa). This s perhaps all right if the interstate differences on the omitted side are not large. In India, this is not the case, and hence all the FC formulae for tax sharing have tried to take into account both sides in recent times.

On the revenue capacity side, only variants of the income criterion have been used in India. Our assessment shows several shortcomings of the actual variables used. Which make it more prudent to use them, if at all, with a much smaller weight than actually assigned in recent times. Infact, a direct assessment of relative revenue capacity is both possible and desirable; given that this can be accomplished at varying levels of complexity, a suitable balance between transparency and comprehensiveness can be struck.

On the expenditure needs side, sever variables have been used, but with progressively declining weights. The peculiar requirement of using only 1971 population may be partly responsible for the declining weight; else, we think it deserves much higher weight. We also think that the population data have not been used to maximum effect, the use of the details available could significantly improve the formula in particular an index of the percentage of population requiring special attention of the government (scheduled castes, scheduled tribes children below a certain age, senior citizens, the seriously disabled) could be a very good indicator of expenditure needs. Including such a variable in the distribution formula with reasonable weight would strengthen equalization and allow the weight on population per se to be reduced. Care has to be taken to select variables that are not out comes of government policy to avoid problems relating to moral hazard (this is the reason we are critical of the poverty criterion). Geographical features like area, and other characterisitics that may cause cost disabilities (e.g. hilly terrain) are also assessed to be appropriate, although it is necessary to take into account the costs associated with highly congested urban areas too. Criteria like an infrastructure index are best avoided, primarily due to incentive problems: instead need based variables ought to be used.

The FCs have superimposed fiscal performance indicators on the other two types of indicators discussed above. These are in principle bad criteria to be determining transfers, and can be justified only as temporary ones called in to service for the fighiong operations, in the context of all round deficits. Even if the latter was the case, a simplistic variable representing revenue balance would actually only be counter equalizing and appropriate multiple indicator based criterion has to be devised.

Finally, we believe that any significant transfers based on the origin of tax revenues is not logically maintainable; however there is a case for a small amount to be transferred on this basis of an approximation thereof.

2

Restructuring Public Finances

Introduction

The structural imbalance in India's public finance system has existed right from the beginning. While the deterioration in fiscal turning points in the last decade can be related to some proximate causes like pay revision of employees or sluggish revenue growth because of a slowdown in the economy, the imbalances in the state budgets have their origin in factors that are structural in character (Anand, Bagchi and Sen 2001). The main objective of this paper is to suggest restructuring of public finances of the centre and state governments to provide macroeconomic stability, equitable growth in the country and improve efficiency of resources. The paper also suggests ways to argument revenue resources. The paper also suggests ways to augment revenue resources and contraction in expenditure.

Public finance in India are at inflection point. If past data is analysed and projected in future there would be little hope of seeing any improvement in any of the major macroeconomic indicators. The Eleventh Finance Commission (EFC), which was entrusted with the responsibility of suggesting restructuring of the central and state governments public finances, had envisaged trend path for level of revenue and fiscal deficit, the level of debt and expenditure on social infrastructure. None of the indicators seem to be on the trend-path and gap between the suggested path and actual turnout has stubbornly remained.

Given the objective of this paper, section II analyses suggestions made by the EFC. Section III compares the EFC projections with most recent data available, Section IV describes the restructuring process at the national and sub-national level. Section V examines whether the gradual restructuring process and institutional changes are going to have a favourable impact on the macroeconomic indicators in medium term. Based on assumptions on GDP growth rate, inflation and interest rates. Three scenarios have been outlined in Section VI to estimate the economic outcome In the coming decade. Finally, in Section VII suggestions are mad on restructure public finances to meet development objectives of the economy.

Restructuring Suggested by Eleventh Finance Commission

For the first time the terms of reference of a Finance Commission was enlarged to suggest the restructuring of public finances. Clause 4 of the TOR required the Eleventh finance commission (EFC) "to review the sate of finance of the union and the sates and suggest ways and means by which the governments, collectively and severally, may bring about a restructuring of the public finances so as to restore budgetary balance and maintain macroeconomic stability. The commission considered and spelt out the relevant parameters of macroeconomic stability specified a restructuring path and gave an outline by which such restructuring can be brought about by the central and state governments" (GOI 2000).

This changed the scope of the Finance Commission work and it recommended fiscal transfers which shall bring about macroeconomic stability over the medium term Probably it was in response to the shift in emphasis from planned allocation to market-based allocation of resources. Central as well as state governments used (misused) all the financing measure which could soften the budget constraint in 1990s. Resources were raised using state guarantees without due diligence process. Temporary financial instruments such as ways and Means advances and overdraft from RBI, which are essentially bridge loans, were used to finance projects which require long-term funds. The misuse of such facilities gave rise to liquidity mismatch and forced the central bank to tighten the norms for providing Ways and Means facility as well as for guarantees (RBI 2002 and 2003C).

The EFC recognized upfront that general government fiscal deficit is too high and it needed to be controlled and the government should go all out to reduce the fiscal deficit. I underlined the importance of having surpluses on revenue account to finance capital expenditure but the growing demand of servicing of past debt has meant that the revenue deficit could not be reined in. Failing to raise revenue receipt resulted in self perpetuating spiral of debt and deficit, and threatened the macroeconomic stability.

The term macroeconomic stability was defined as

stability of prices at full employment of available resources generally referred to as non-accelerating inflation rate of unemployment (NAIRU) in economic literature. However, this would provide only internal balance and for the external balance it was suggested that the current account deficit should be within limits which can be serviced in the long run out of export earnings and factor incomes form abroad. The commission also suggested that fiscal policy should be counter cyclical to economic fluctuations in order to maintain stability in short-term. To achieve long-run stability the composition of government expenditure ,debt and fiscal deficit should be in line with potential full employment output. The report acknowledged the limit placed on magnetized deficit through the MOU between the GOI and the RBI however it suggested that the limit should be linked to GDP. While considering sustainability of domestic debt, it was emphasized that budget constraint rule—the rate of interest should not exceed the rate of GDP growth should be followed. The report emphasized that this rule is violated in the budgets of center, in the combined accounts of the center and states and individually in many states (Para 3.14).

Fiscal deficit also came under scrutiny and a view was taken that fiscal deficit as a proportion of (full employment) GDP depends on how the borrowed funds are used. Nevertheless, revenue budget should generate surpluses for government investment. While discussing normative level of fiscal deficit, the report suggested the same norm prevalent in the EU countries under the Maastricht treaty for fiscal deficit and inflation. The fiscal deficit of 3 percent of GDP and the debt-GDP ratio of less than 60 percent are the EU norms. For a growing economy like that of India, the EFC recommended that debt-gdp ratio should be stabilized around 55 per cent and a combined fiscal deficit of the center and states at 6.5 percent of GDP.

While emphasis remained on control of fiscal deficit, the report was emphatic that the tax base must be expanded to increase tax revenue so that fiscal compression does not hurt expenditure on social and infrastructure sectors. While recognizing vertical imbalance of India federal structure, the Commission was emphatic to devolve taxation power to state and local bodies so that expenditure and revenue collection gap narrows down to some extent (Para 3.74). In order to achieve fiscal consolidation the commission recommended the following important institutional changes at the central and state level.

Central Government

(a) Widening of the tax base and listing of services in the concurrent list.

(b) Rightsizing of the government at all levels.

(c) Prescribe limits on borrowings as proportion of GDP.

(d) Revise the present system of determining and providing assistance for state plans.

(e) Introduce a multi-year budgeting process.

State Government

(a) Use profession tax and tax farm incomes to augment tax revenues of states.

(b) Rely on user shares reflective of input casts to augment non tax revenue.

(c) Rightsizing of the government at all levels.

(d) Prescribe limits on borrowings as proportion of GSDP

(e) Introduce a multi-year budgeting process.

Review of EFC Recommendations

Central Government

On the basis of point estimates projected by the EFC one can safety conclude that except inflation rate and current balance all other indicators are too far from the EFC projection for 2004-05 and it is unlikely that these targets can be achieved (Table 1). One can even argue that had the economy been operating near its full potential, not only the twin deficits could have been reined in, the turnout would have been very near the EFC projections without affecting inflation and current account balance adversely.

Table 1: Macro Scenario Over 1999-04 and EFC's Projection from 2004–05

	1999-2000	*2000-01*	*2001-02*	*2002-03*	*2003-04 (BE)/(F)*	*2004-05 (EFC Proj)*
Growth rate (% per annum)	6.1	4.4	5.6	4.3	6.5	7.0-7.5
Inflation rate (% per annum)	3.3	7.2	3.6	3.4	3.5	5.5-5.0
Current account balance (% of GDP)	-1.1	-0.8	0.2	0.7	1.0	-1.5
Revenue deficit (% of GDP)	6.4	6.8	7.2	7.0	6.1	1.0
Fiscal deficit (% of GDP)	9.9	9.9	9.8	9.4	9.5	6.5
Tax revenue (% of GDP)	14.1	14.6	13.7	14.9	15.2	16.7

Non-tax revenue (% of GDP)	3.8(2.5)	3.5	4.1	4.7	4.4	3.2
Capital expenditure (% of GDP)	3.3(4.2)	3.1	3.2	3.9	4.4	6.6

Notes: Figures in brackets are the EFC's base figures where there is a significant change from the actual data excludes interest paying from states to centre. F -forecast.

Source: RBI (2003a), RBI (2003b), Budget Papers.

Graph 1

Central Government Repayment Schedule of Domestic Debt (August 2003)

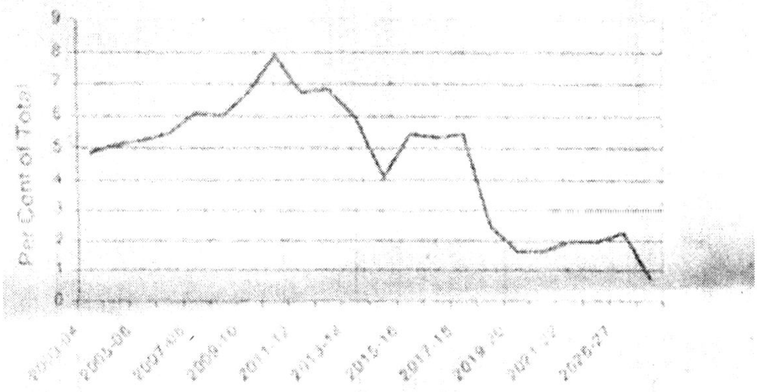

Table 2: Tax Revenues 1999-04 and EFC's Projection for 2004-05

	1999-2000	*2000-01*	*2001-02*	*2002-03*	*2003-04 (BE)*	*2004-05 (EFC Proj)*
Income Tax	1.5	1.8	1.6	1.7	1.8	1.8
Corporation tax	1.7	2.0	1.9	2.0	2.1	2.2
Union excise duties	3.5	3.7	3.6	3.9	3.9	3.7
Custom duties	2.7	2.6	2.1	2.0	2.0	2.6
Central taxes (gross)	9.6	10.3	9.4	9.8	10.1	10.3
States own tax revenues	5.2	5.6	5.6	5.9	6.0	6.4

Source: RBI (2003b), RBI (2003b), Budget Papers.

Table 2 shows that barring custom duties and states own tax revenues, other major tax sources are nearly in line with the set target. Reduction in custom duties is in line with opening up of manufacturing sector to international competition by lowering tax barriers.

Graph 2

Interest Rate Profile of Central Government Debt (March 31, 2003)

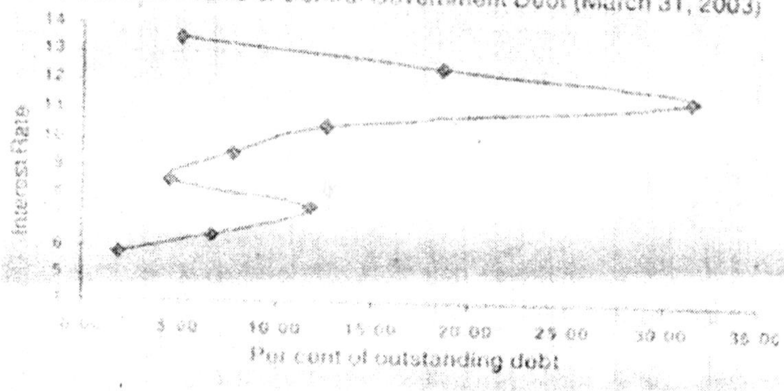

Combined finances of the center and states show sizeable divergence from the EFC projections of revenue deficit, fiscal deficit and capital expenditure. Revenue expenditure could not be controlled and, hence, weight of adjustment fell on capital expenditure. Tax revenue, non-tax revenue and revenue receipts suggest some improvement over the years and yet are short of the EFC target (Table 3).

Table 3: Fiscal Parameters Center and States: 1999-04 EFC's Projection for 2004-05

	1999-2000	*2000-01*	*2001-02*	*2002-03*	*2003-04 (BE)*	*2004-05 (EFC Proj)*
	Combined Finance					
Tax revenues	14.1	14.6	13.7	14.9	15.2	16.7
Non–tax revenues	3.8(2.5)	3.5	4.1	4.7	4.4	3.2
Revenue receipts	19.4(16.6)	19.4	19.1	20.9	21.0	20.0

Revenue expenditure	26.3(23.3)	26.6	26.7	28.3	27.5	21.0
Capital expenditure	3.3(4.2)	3.1	3.2	3.9	4.4	6.6
Revenue deficit	6.4(6.8)	6.8	7.2	7.0	6.1	1.0
Fiscal deficit	9.9	9.9	9.8	9.4	9.5	6.5
		Centre				
Tax revenues	8.8	9.0	8.1	9.0	9.2	10.0
Non-tax revenues	2.8	2.7	3.0	2.9	2.5	3.0
Revenue receipts	9.4(11.5)	9.2	8.8	9.6	9.3	13.3
Revenue expenditure	12.9(13.1)	13.2	13.1	13.8	13.4	11.5
Capital expenditure	2.5(2.6)	2.3	2.7	2.5	2.7	4.0
Revenue deficit	3.5(3.8)	4.1	4.4	4.2	4.1	1.0
Fiscal deficit	5.4(3.6)	5.7	6.1	5.9	5.6	4.5
		States				
Tax revenues	5.3	5.6	5.6	5.9	6.0	4
Non-tax revenues	1.5(1.0)	1.5	1.4	1.5	1.4	1.5
Revenue receipts	10.4	8.8	8.6	9.0	9.2	13.0
Revenue expenditure	13.3	11.6	11.4	11.7	11.1	13.0
Capital expenditure	2.1	3.1	3.2	3.9	4.4	2.9
Revenue deficit	3.0	2.8	2.8	2.7	2.0	0.0
Fiscal deficit	4.7	4.3	4.2	4.7	4.0	2.5

Source: RBI (2003a), RBI (2003b), Budget Papers.

Graph 3

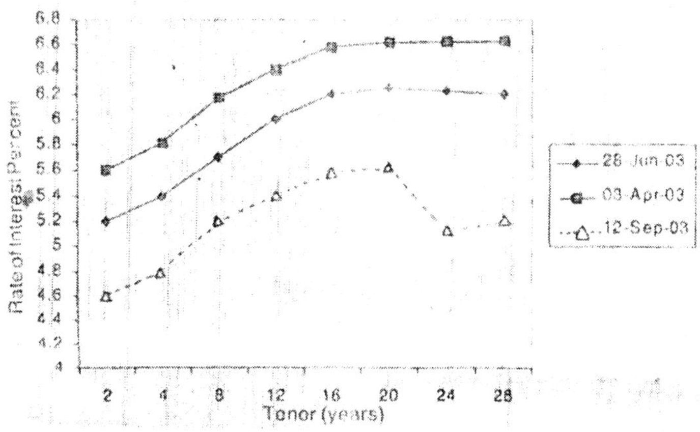

At the centre, revenue expenditure has remained almost at the same level as it was in the base year 1999-2000. As a result, revenue deficits could not be reduced sufficiently. With revenue deficit remaining intractable, there is no reduction in fiscal deficits Consequently capital expenditure which was expected to show a growth of one and a half percentage points of GDP has remained stagnant at the 1999-2000 level as proportion of GDP (Table4)

Table 4: Main Component of Expenditure: 1999-04 EFC's Projection for 2004-05

	1999-2000	*2000-01*	*2001-02*	*2002-03*	*2003-04 (BE)*	*2004-05 (EFC Proj)*
	Revenue expenditure					
	Centre					
Interest payments	5.2(4.7)	5.2	5.1	5.1	5.0	4.3
Pensions	0.8	0.8	0.7	0.6	0.6	0.7
Other general services	0.3(2.5)	0.4	0.4	0.4	0.3	2.1
Social services	0.4	0.3	0.3	0.3	0.3	0.3
Economic service	0.4	0.5	0.4	0.5	0.5	0.3
	States					
Interest payments	2.6(2.3)	2.8	3.2	3.3		2.6
Pensions	1.3(1.2)	1.3	1.3	1.3	n.a	1.0
Other general services	0.1(1.6)	0.2	0.2	0.4	n.a	1.7
Social services of which	5.8(5.1)	5.4	5.6	5.4	n.a	5.8
Education sports etc	3.2	3.1	3.1	2.9	n.a	1.8
Primary health etc	0.9	0.8	0.8	0.8	n.a	0.5
Water supply & sanitation	0.4	0.3	0.3	0.	n.a	0.5
Economic services of	4.3(2.9)	3.3	3.3	3.1	n.a	2.3
which energy						
Capital expenditure		0.7	0.8	0.6	n.a	
Center	2.5(2.6)	2.3	2.7	2.5	2.7	4.0
States	2.1	3.1	3.2	3.9	4.4	2.9

Source: RBI (2003a), RBI (2003b), Budget Papers.

State Governments

That the states own tax revenues potential has not been fully exploited is evident from the economic data. However, the gap is narrow enough which can be easily filled. Revenue deficit of the combined state finances has been gradually declining but fiscal deficit remained stubbornly above 4 percent of GDP (Table 3). Capital expenditure of the states since 2000-01 has shown an unusual spurt due to compensation as suggested by their respective state finance commissions (RBI 2003). But revenue receipts have fallen short significantly from the EFC's target of 2004-05 which is closely related to the revenue deficit of the states (Table 3).

Interest payments on debt have been rising rather declining as expected by the EFC. Expenditure on economic services remained high though declining in the last couple of years. Interestingly, expenditure under energy head is expected to decline in 2002-03 (BE) (Table 4).

In brief, at the center, interest payments could not be reined in and it remained a major component of revenue expenditure. At sates level, interest payments have been growing. Expenditure on social services which was envisioned to grow by 0.7 percent of GDP has shrunk by 0.4 percent of GDP over by 2002-03.

Emerging Pattern of Restructuring Process

Table 1 shows that the decline in tax collection as well as the economic growth were in the region of 0.5-0.6 and 2-2.5 percentage points respectively (Table 1) Nevertheless, restructuring on various fronts, in line with the EFC recommendations continued, albeit slowly, and many of them have reached fruition in the current year.

We outline the monetary and structural changes and their implications on fiscal health of the government finances in the coming years.

Central Government

The weak links—a narrow tax base and overwhelming dependence on manufacturing sector for tax revenues-in the central government finance continue to persist, despite various measurers taken to strengthen the process of fiscal consolidation. The union budget for 2003-04, in particular, has attempted to address the issues of structural weaknesses in the central government finances. The budget has projected a modest growth in revenue collection and larger non-debt capital mobilization through disinvestments. The rationalization of expenditure and improved cash management suggested in the budget would consolidate public expenditure and enhance productive use of financial resources. Investments in infrastructure sectors are envisaged through public–private partnership. The initiatives such as prepayment of external debt, buy-back of past high cost loans form the banking system and debt-swapping with state governments are expected to strengthen the fiscal consolidation process. Fiscal Responsibility and Budget Management (FRBM) Act, 2003: Bringing fiscal responsibility on statute books is a landmark legislation and its implementation over the next few years will have some impact on public finances. In particular, bringing revenue deficit to zero by march 31, 2008 is a stiff target. Compliance with the act has already started in earnest (Article 7) and one can hope that medium term fiscal targets advocated in the act are kept in mind during budget making process in the fiscal year 2004-05 which would be the first FY under the FRBM Act.

The center armed with this act can now fend off unreasonable pressure form states for assistance. The act has bestowed total responsibility to RBI in matters related to monetary affairs of the government.

Restructuring of debt: Following a softening interest rate regime the government has initiated debt restructuring process on three fronts, viz. pre-payment of external debt, buy-back of loans form banks contracted under high interest rate regime and debt-swapping scheme with the state governments. With regard to external debt repayment, the government has effected premature repayment of high cost currency pool loans of the World Bank and of the Asian Development Bank, totaling around $3 billion, taking advantage of comfortable foreign exchange reserves and lower domestic interest rates. The 2003-04 budget has reaffirmed the intention to continue with the policy of prudently managing the external liabilities and of proactively liquidating relatively higher cost component of external debt portfolio.

As regards domestic debt, the measures are initiated on the context of large proportion of central government domestic debt contracted under the high interest rate regime, which is thinly traded and largely owned by public sector banks and institutions. With the softening of interest rates, such loans commanded a premium over their face value (Graph 1 and 2) under the debt buy-back scheme, the central government offered to buy-back high interest loans from banks on voluntary basis. The scheme enabled the banks to improve their liquidity position by encashing the premium for making provisions for their NPAs. Furthermore, in case the banks declare the premium received as business income, for income tax purpose, they will be allowed additional deduction to the extent such income is used for provisioning of their NPAs for improving their balance sheet.

The process of debt restructuring is being carried out in full earnest. The RBI has been able to raise money at interest rates which are historically low. For instance, 10 year money has been raised at 5.7 percent for the centre and 6.2 percent for the states (Graph 3). In the first quarter of FY 2003-04 the central government had a freak result where its fiscal deficit has been lower than the revenue deficit due to states repaying Rs.24268 crore of their debt.

Utilization of Divestment Windfall: The Efc had recommended that proceeds from disinvestments process should be used to retire debt. Since 1999-2000, proceeds from divestment including control premium, dividend and dividend tax et. Have not been substantial as percentage of GDP (Table A4). But, thee was a distinct change in disinvestments process and government policy. Unlike previous disinvestments of PSUS, the emphasis was on selling government equity to a strategic buyer with management control in a transparent manner using market intermediaries for pricing of assets, marketing of the strategic stake, etc.

During the disinvestments of BALCO, the Supreme Court gave the landmark judgment that disinvestments could be effected by an executive order which would have made the future disinvestments of the rest of the PSUs simpler and faster. The policy of disinvestments specifically aims at modernization and upgradation of PSEs, creation of new assets, generation of employment, and retiring of public debt. Further , the then finance minister in his Budget Speech for 2003-04 announced that "the pace of disinvestments will accelerate in the coming year. I wish to also state that details about the already announced Disinvestments Fund and Asset management company, to hold residual shares post disinvestments, shall be finalised early in 2003-04 disinvestments is not merely for mobilizing revenues for the government, it is mainly for unlocking the productive potential of these undertakings, and for reorienting the government away form business strategic sale of many PSUs since January 2000 corroborates the previous government intent (table A5). The new government has announced that it is not in favour of divestment of profit making PSUs. To what an extent the government would be able to raise resources by sale of sick PSUs is yet to be tested in the market place.

The disinvestments process and schedule is now on a slippery ground as the Supreme court's judgement on the sale of HPCL and BPCL requires that disinvestments of PSUs created by a legislative act or paid from consolidated fund of the government requires approval form the respective legislature. This would add to the traditional problems related to valuation and labour policy. Moreover, lack of political will may dry the disinvestments windfall gains.

State Governments

Medium-terms fiscal reforms programmes The EFC had recommended the establishment of an incentive fund to encourage speedier fiscal reforms in the states which can be easily monitored and the span of the programme should be over the EFC time frame. In response to this, the central government created the states. Fiscal reforms Facility (2000-01 to 2004-05). An incentive fund of Rs.10607 crore over the EFCs lifetime was allocated. To be eligible to draw from the fund, states having revenue deficit were to reduce it by five percentage points as a proportion of the state's total revenue receipts in each year till 2004-05. states were also allowed to rouse resources from the market to meet their structural adjustment requirement arising from VRS. Downsizing of PSEs and center state debt swap for bringing down interest liabilities (GOI 2002).

In response to this 16 states drew up a Medium Term Fiscal Reforms programme (MTFRP) and signed a MOU with the MOF. GOI The objective of MTFRP is to eliminate revenue deficit to reduce fiscal deficit to sustainable levels and to reduce debt GDP ratio including contingent liabilities to sustainable levels. The MTFRP includes a whole gamut of fiscal consolidation measures, PSUs restructuring , power sector reforms, etc. In line with the EFC's recommendations, the Planning commission is ensuring that the Annual Plan framework is consistent with the MTFRP.

Reforms in Power sector. Fiscal reform s of the states are in extricably intertwined with power sector reforms. Commercial losses of the SEBs mounted to 1.2 percent of GDP in 2000-01 (Ro 2002) in comparison to this fiscal deficit of states was 4.3 percent of GDP in 2000-01 and it is expected to be 4 percent in 2003-04 (Table 3) The Electricity Act 2003 consolidates laws relating to transmission, distribution, trading and use of electricity. The act is the most important legislative change for he power sector but the other two reports, namely, Expert Committee Reports—Settlement of SEB Dues Chaired by Montek Singh Ahluwalia (GOI 2001) and Structuring of Accelerated Power Development and Reform Project (APDRP) : Reform Framework and principles of Financial Restructuring of SEBs chaired by Deepak Parekh (GOI

2002a) are more important in the near future for state finances.

It was in 2000 that central and state governments realize the debilitating effect of SEBs on power sector development. The GOI proposed a scheme to restructure finances of the SEBs (GOI 2001). The crux of the scheme is that past dues of the SEBs cease to be a financial burden on the SEBs and have to be serviced by the respective state governments to concessional terms. The future revenue generation of SEBS s therefore no longer hostage to past liabilities and hence, the path to reform is smoother Additionally, I the debt forgiveness that the One Time Settlement of Dues entitled MoUs which were signed by the state governments, committed them to reform including tariff convergence. This will nudge state governments to reform their power sector.

Implementation of the one time settlement of SEB dues: Under this scheme the government of India, the Reserve Bank of India and the state governments signed tripartite agreements. The RBI notified in July 2003 that the statewise dues of around Rs. 12.000 crore is to be paid by Andhra Pradesh, Assam, Goa, Gujarat, Himachal Pradesh, Haryana, Karnatak, Kerala, Meghalaya, Nagaland, Punjab, Rajasthan, Tamilnadu, Uttar Pradesh, Uttaranchal, West Bengal to NTPC and other central public sector undertaking (CPSUs). The states which did not figure in the RBI's notification were Maharashtra, Madhya Pradesh, Chhattisgarh, Bihar, Jharkhand, Orissa, Sikkim and Jammu and Kashmir. Since then, the Maharashtra government has signed a tripartite agreement with the ministry of power and the Reserve Bank of India (RBI) or one-time settlement of dues of around Rs. 600 crore owed by Maharashtra State Electricity Board (MSEB) to various CPSUs (RBI 2003b).

Under the one-time settlement of SEB dues, the debt burden of SFBs has been further reduced as the central sector power utilities have waived Rs.10,000 crore delayed payment surcharge component payable by defaulting state electricity boards. Accordingly, total SFB dues to be securities through the issue of tax free bonds by the concerned state governments has reduced to Rs. 31000 crore from Rs. 41000 crore (the Economic times July 29,2003)

Further, the central government- owned Power Finance Corporation (PFC) has restructured debts of around Rs. 800 crore of 18 state owned utilities . The state utilities are expected to take advantage of the debt restructuring because PFC reduced its base lending rate to nine percent in June 2003. The debt restructuring would reduce the interest burden on the states taking up power sector reforms. Past loans were give @ 12-15 percent anum. Restructuring, since the utilities continue to suffer revenue shortfalls. PFC could offer this restructuring package to the states as it took advantage of the soft interest rate regime by effecting prepayments and exercising early exit options on some of its high cost borrowings, particularly bonds (*Business Line,* July 24, 2003).

Accelerated power development and restructuring programme (APDRP): The Parekh Committee Report outlined a reform framework and principles of financial restructuring of SEBs that could form the basis for devising state specific reform programmes. The report is aimed at helping the states to devise strategies that are credible and hence, bankable for raising transition financing support as recommended by the Ahluwalia Committee (GOI 2001). The Parekh Committee decided to address its task in two stages. In the first stage the committee reviewed the Accelerate Power Development Programme and suggested measures for improvement to be incorporated in the APDRP as part of a consolidated reform approach; and evolved a reform framework and broad principles for the financial restructuring of SEBs, based on a review of reform experiences I on India and abroad. There form framework has four critical components market structure, distribution zoning, regulatory approach and ownership. The report has not suggested any specific way to reorganize a SEB. A reform template is given in the report which will be the starting point for devising the state specific reforms the second stage of the committee's work.

Implementation of APDRP: All states had been requested last year to draw up their five year programme for the power sector. The allocation under the APDRP depends on the states; performance for both components of the programme incentives and investment. It is interesting to note that almost all states have drawn up plans to invest money in power projects. Though investment component of APDRP has achieved its budget target, states have not been able to tie up their counter part funds. Only 4 percent of target investment could be utilized (Table A11).

Most state governments have now realized that power reforms have to be implemented to save the bleeding SEBs. For example, in 2003-04, Rajasthan and Delhi have accepted the tariff orders of the State Electricity Regulatory Commission and implemented tariff hikes. In 2002-03, Madhya Pradesh affected steep tariff hikes while Tamilnadu and Punjab introduced tariff on agricultural power consumption.

Nevertheless, there is still a wide gap between cost of supply and the average tariff. The gap widened from 0.23/kwh in 1992-93 to Rs. 1.10/kwh in 2001-02. But, it is showing some signs of reversal with decrease in the gap to Rs.0.91/kwh in 2002-03. Apart from setting up of SERCs the states power reform measures include reducing T and D losses by 5 percent annually, unbundling, 100 percent consumer metering and achieving parity between cost of power and tariffs. In consumer metering, Delhi, Haryana, Himachal Pradesh, Karnataka, Kerala and Tamil Nadu have achieved 100 percent metering. There are only three states which have below 50 percent metering—Sikkim, Mizoram and J. and K. Majority of the states managed to achieve over 80 percent metering by December 2002. Nearly 22 states have setup power regulatory commission and many have proposed unbundling and corporatisation of SEBs.

The finance ministry's review of MTFRP indicates that growth in gross subsidy and commercial losses have been marginally arrested with a corresponding increase I revenue mobilization in the power sector. Gross power subsidy has come down from Rs. 34587 crore in 2001-02 to Rs. 33280 crore in 2002-03 and is further expected to go down to Rs. 32429 crore in the current fiscal. The reducing trend in subsidy has been attributed to increase in tariffs to agricultural consumer and implementation of State electricity Regulatory Commissions' tariff awards.

Accelerated irrigation benefits programme (AIBP): a large number of river valley projects, both multipurpose and irrigation have spilled over from plan to plan mainly because of financial constraints being faced by the state governments. As a result of this, despite a huge investment having already been made on these projects, the desired benefits have not accrued to the economy. There were 171 major, 259 medium and 72 extension/renovation/modernization (ERM) of on going irrigation projects in the country at various stages of construction at the end of the Eighth Plan (i.e. end of March, 1997) with a spill over cost of Rs.75690crore. Under the AIBP, the union government took remedial measures for expeditious completion of some of the projects which were in the advanced stage of completion.

Irrigation subsidies area substantial part of state budgets and, therefore, wide ranging organizational reforms are on the agenda of several states: AP, Orissa and Tamil Nadu have enacted legislation envisaging major changes in the organization for water development. Some—notably Andhra Pradesh and Maharashtra—have taken significant and bold steps to raise water rates. Andhra Pradesh has legislated water user participation at all levels of each major and medium irrigation system. Maharashtra also has water user associations. Entrusting maintenance and repair to the local water user associations rather than contractors has given a strong sense of involvement on the part of users resulting in speedier completion of works, at lower cost and better quality than under the earlier dispensation (Vaidyanathan 2003; WB 2002).

Non-recurring revenue avenues (divestment of state PSUs): Recommendations of the EFC apply to state level public enterprises (SLPE) as much as to central public sector undertakings. Divestment process at state level has not been encouraging, though some states are gearing upto disinvest/close loss making enterprises in an accelerated manner (Table A6). Andhra Pradesh, Gujarat, Karnataka and Maharashtra account for more than 50 percent of total investment in SLPEs and except Maharashtra the other three states are pursuing restructuring/disinvestments of SLPE earnestly (Table A7). It is disheartening to note that Punjab, Rajasthan, UP and West Bengal which account for approximately 25 percent of total investment in SLPEs, the process of disinvestments is moving at a snail's speed. Disinvestments process in Punjab has gathered pace recently and may gain momentum in the coming years.

The restructuring of SLPEs is part of the states MTFRP. It is worth noting that SLPEs run with periodical infusion of capital in the form of fresh share capital form the state governments or additional loans from them. This is mainly due to the running down of net worth though regular losses. In this situation, when states have to finance their deficit, they often force repayment of loans or payment of accumulated interest due to them consequently, it leaves the SLPEs with little productive capital, further worsening their financial health (Sen 2000). Therefore disinvestments of SLPEs should be seen as reduction in recurring cost (staff cost, establishment cost, etc.) due to perennial losses being made by these SLPEs rather than as avenues to raise resources.

Restructuring of debt : Many states have passed fiscal responsibility act and are restructuring debt in coordination with the central government. In states, revenue expenditure accounts for a large proportion of the aggregate expenditure and interest payment accounts for roughly 25 percent of the revenue receipts. In some states interest payments have exceeded 30 percent of the revenue receipts. To meet redemption of market loans of states the RBI set up a consolidated Sinking fund in 1999-2000 and also allowed states to directly access the market for resources ranging from 5 percent to 35 percent of gross borrowings, with the states deciding on the method, timing and maturities of the borrowings. These facilities have enabled the states to reduce their loan and advances requirements from the centre. States have also reduced their loans and advances extended for non development purposes. The weighted average of interest rate on market borrowings of states has declined continuously in the recent years from 14 percent in 1995-96 to 7.49 percent in 2002–03 (GOI 2002). Outstanding guarantees of state governments have reduced from 8 percent of GDP in 2001 to 7.2 percent in 2002 (RBI 2003a).

The net market borrowing of states has been declining and growth has been arrested after a spurt I growth in 2001-02 (Table A8) but long-end of the market loans is building up rapidly and repayment after 2007-08 is growing at an unsustainable rate (Table A9). Under MTFRP states will extinguish their central government loans bearing interest rate greater than 13 percent by 2005-2006 but loans with 12 percent 13 percent coupon rates amount to almost one-quarter of their total loans, though overwhelmingly these are central government loans to states (Table A10, Graph 4 and 5).

Graph 4

State Government Repayment Schedule (Per Cent of Total)

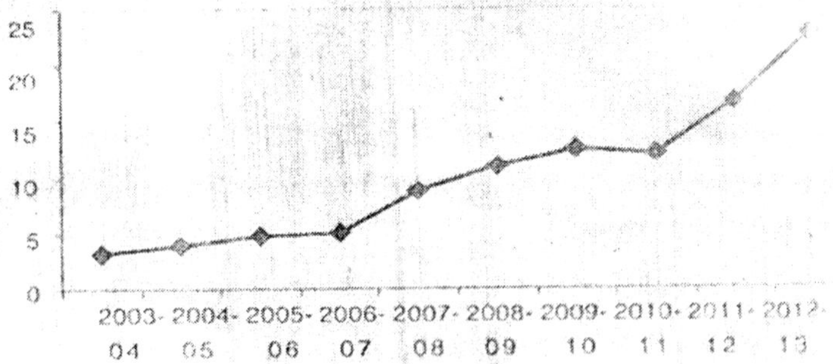

Graph 5

Interest Rate Profile of State Governments Debt

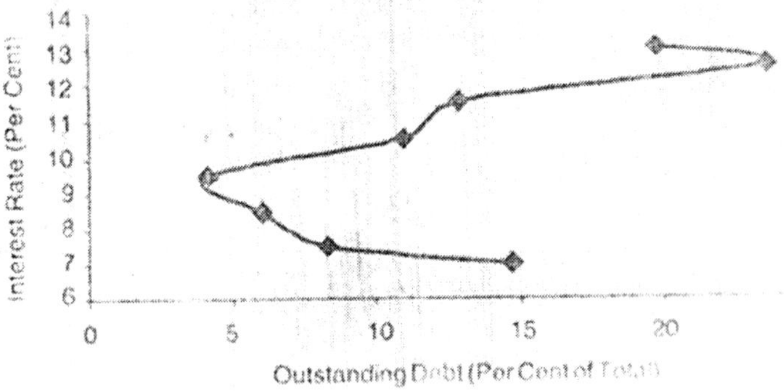

Recent developments : under the debt swap scheme between the central government and the states, all state loans to the government of India bearing coupons in excess of 13 percent would be swapped (of the total stock of debt of Rs. 244000 crore owed by the states to the government of India as on March 31, 2002, a little over Rs. 1,00,000 crore bear coupon rates in excess of 13 percent per annum) over three year period ending in 2005-06. It is envisaged that 2 percent, 30 percent and 40 percent of small savings funds will be used to retire high cost debt bearing more than 13 percent rate of interest and by 2005-06 all high cost debt will get swapped. The states are expected to save an estimated Rs.81000 crore in interest, and deferred loan repayments, over the residual maturity period of the loans (RBI 2003a). To provide extra resources to states the central government is going to transfer the entire proceeds of small savings to the states. The scheme would also help to restrain the debt build-up in states through the small savings scheme. Further, interest rates on small savings as well as on states plan loans were reduced by 50 basis points.

At the same time the RBI has raised the maximum tenor of state government loans to 12 years form 10 years. All state governments have been offered to sell 'on-tap' 6.2 percent state development loan maturing on august 25,2015. It makes good economic sense to lengthen the average maturity of loans when interest rates are low.

Reforms at Local Government Level

Local bodies are responsible for drinking water, street lighting and local roads. 73rd and 74th A amendments have expanded their expenditure responsibilities without providing for commensurate power to raise resources. Local bodies in turn have looked for concessional loans from state governments or have abdicated responsibilities to departmental agencies operated by state governments. Most of the states constituted second finance commission to suggest funds transfer to local government bodies. Some states are in the process of constituting third finance commission Accounting reforms and property tax reforms are important developments in locals government sector.

Assessment of Restructuring Process

Analysis of public finances trend of recent past makes a bleak reading and on the face of hard evidence of past data there is no confirmation of restructuring of the EFC were implemented and government, both at the center and states, are carrying on their business as usual. A generous critique could say that present governments are victim of their predecessors' misdeeds. Nothing could be further from the truth. One of the factors which prevented hard evidence of structural changes to be noticeable was that the economy operated below its full capacity.

In restructuring public finances, the EFC emphasized that the level of debt was unsustainable and fiscal deficit should be pared to 6.5 percent of GDP by 2004-05 (par 3.18); the government expenditure should be counter cyclical to economic growth and expenditure on social infrastructure should be raised from 2.1 percent of GDP in 1999-2000 to 2.9 percent of GDP by 2004-05 (Table 4). We assess the impact of the restructuring process on these three critical areas.

Level of Debt and Twin Deficits

Analysis of public finance carried out by academics and international rating agencies and recent data on public finances provide no comfort on the progress of controlling twin deficits revenue and fiscal s suggested in the EFC report. In particular the government has failed miserably in controlling revenue and fiscal deficits. But considering that the economy was operating far below its potential between fiscal year 1999-2000 to FY 2002-03, the twin deficit may have provided counter cyclical weight to the economy which may have resulted in gradual increase of deficits. Revenue targets as percentage of GDP were met but expenditure did not, mainly because interest outgo as percentage of GDP could not be reduced. The losses in power sector alone constitute well over 25 percent of total revenue deficits. These losses may reduce to 0.158 percent of GDP by 2006-07, if states are able to implement their respective Financial Turnround Plan submitted to the ministry of power under our business as usual scenario.

A detailed analysis of institutional changes, restructuring of domestic and foreign debts, favourable macroeconomic conditions low rate of inflation and interest rate—suggest that public finances are on the turning point. Conversion of ad-hoe treasury bills into dated securities illustrate that magnetization is under control as envisaged in the MOU between the RBI and the central government to eliminate the use of ad-hoc treasury bills to finance budget deficits. Repayment schedule for market loans and interest profile of outstanding central government securities reveal that interest burden would peak in 2010-11 in nominal terms but the debt (percent of GDP) is going to reduce substantially as debt on shorter end is getting extinguished rather than growing (Table A2 and A3).

Whereas the EFC included only direct government liabilities in fiscal deficit, Kapur and Patel (2003) included all public sector liabilities including contingent liabilities. It is the centers revenue deficit which is at the center of growing fiscal deficit and to macro manage the economy to ensure stability, adequate fiscal corrections must take place. Burden of adjustment must be shred by the center and states for sustained growth. A sustainable fiscal-financial monetary plan will be a painful one and despite fiscal adjustment undertaken in mid-

1990s solvency is not assured. A primary surplus of four and half percentage points is required to stabilize the debt GDP ratio and long term real growth rate must exceed long term real interest rate by one percentage point to succeed in closing more than half of the primary deficit (Buiter and Patel 1997).

According to Standards and Poor rating agency fiscal deficits and the debt burden of India are worse than the similarly rated countries. It is the gross general government debt/GDP excluding guarantees which have climbed to 84 percent of GDP from the five year average (1998-2002) of approximately 67 percent which is worrisome to the rating agency (Graph 6).

Graph 6

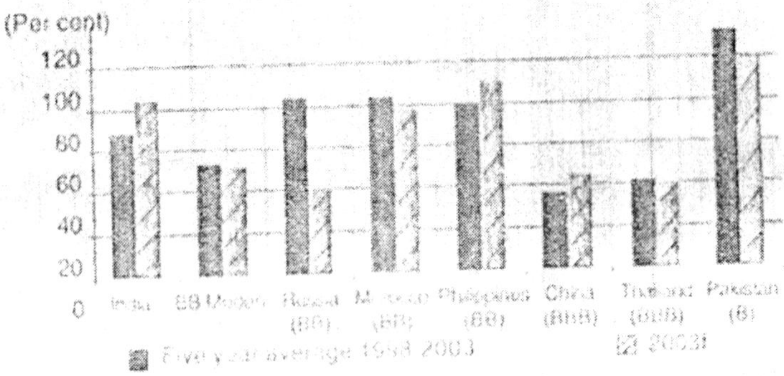

Source: S and P (2003).

Domestic debt in the BB+ rated countries is 45 percent of GDP and fiscal deficit is below 2,5percent of GDP (Graph 6 Gross general government debt/GDP and Graph 7 General Government fiscal Deficit /GDP). In India, in contrast the general government deficits have persistently remained in the range 9 percent 10 percent of GDP in the past few years leading to an erosion of fiscal flexibility (Graph 7).

Graph 7

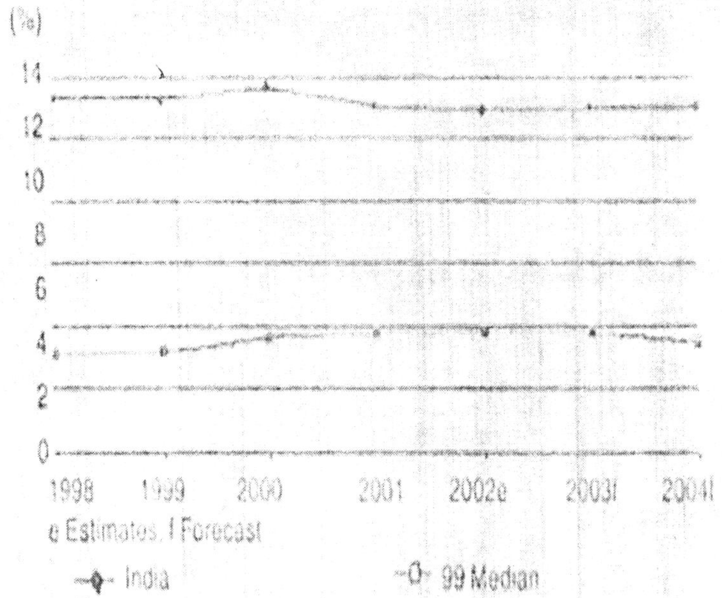

Source: S and P (2003)

The general government guarantees still account for about 11 percent of GDP in March 2002, of which guarantees by state governments alone were 8.1 percept of GDP (S and P 2003).

The size of the external debt burden in India has been falling since fiscal year 2001 because of better access to the credit and lower interest rates in the domestic markets. Total external debt is estimated to fall to US$ 98.7 billion or 117 percent of current account receipts , at the end of fiscal year 2002, from a peak of 338 percent in fiscal 1992. All but 3 percent of external debt is medium and long term debt, making India's external debt payments less vulnerable to the volatility of short-term interest rate (Graph 8 Total External Debt).

Graph 8

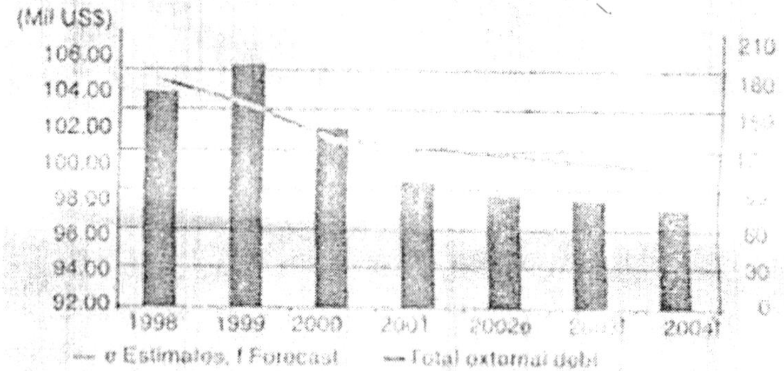

Source: S&P (2003).

The government used reserves to repay expensive multilateral debt. Various private sector firms have also raised domestic debt recently to retire expensive external debt. The general government has become net external creditor from the end of fiscal year 2001.

Nevertheless, the high foreign exchange reserves do not make it easier for the government to pay its debt as payment comes from government revenues ultimately. The reserves make it easier for the government to buy dollars using its rupee revenues in order to service external debt. In the absence of rupee revenues, the government borrowed dollars from the RBI and substituted domestic for external debt. The outstanding liabilities of the public sector – the broadest measure of debt is growing since 1996-97 (Kapur ad Patel 2003). Their calculations show that net total foreign debt has reduced from 35.6 percent of GDP in 1991-92 to 2.5 percent of GDP in 2002-03 whereas net total domestic liabilities over the corresponding period have increased from 46.9 percent to 81.4 percent . Net total liabilities of the public sector which had shrunk to 82.5 percent in 1991-92 to

65.4 percent in 1996-97 have again ballooned to 83.9 percent in 2002-03 (Graph 9- Outstanding liabilities of the public sector (percent of GDP).

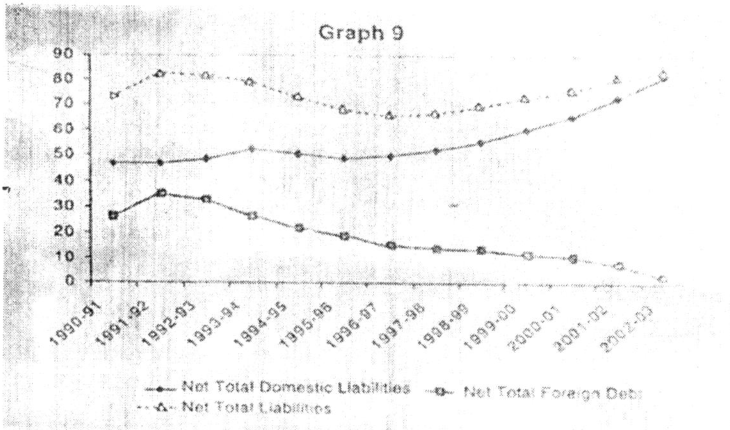

Source: Kapur and Patel (2003).

It is growing net total domestic liabilities at a rapid pace which is worrisome to rating agencies. It is worth nothing that countries have defaulted on their internal debt even when they had sufficient foreign exchange reserves because debt service was taking up too much of government spending and the government decided (as in Russia) to reschedule its debt. Hence, there is little doubt that stock of debt is quite high and retiring of debt gradually is an option which must be explored vigorously.

To provide legislative backing to deficit control, the FRBM Act 2003 is an honest attempt to bring transparency to fiscal governance to the center government level. However, the government is absolved of all its responsibilities if it fails to achieve the pre-announced targets. Thus , the act which could have teeth to gnaw fiscal deficits, has been reduced to a mere statement of intent.

Apart from restructuring of debt to reduce outgo on interest, expenditure needs to be reduced. The Expenditure Review Commission reports on almost all the central government departments to cut wasteful expenditure, however have not been implemented in spirit. Similarly at the state level, notwithstanding the central government's attempts to revive irrigation schemes experience has shown that the present system, whereby the government assumes the responsibility of design, evaluation, financing and construction of irrigation systems as well as their continuing management wholly through its bureaucracy, is in capable of completing the projects in time. The entire process to every stage is far too opaque, open to interference and manipulation, without any effective incentive or mechanism to ensure economical use of resources in construction and management or to ensure that costs are fully recovered.

Counter Cyclical Government Expenditure

The rationale behind counter cyclical government expenditure in that when economic growth I not at its full employment level and there is demand compression at macroeconomic level, the government should be expansive and lean against the wind to decompress demand. He growth in central government market borrowing is take to measure the central government stance to analyse if the government expenditure has been counter cyclical (Graph 10-Growth of Central Government Market Borrowing and GDP).

Graph 10

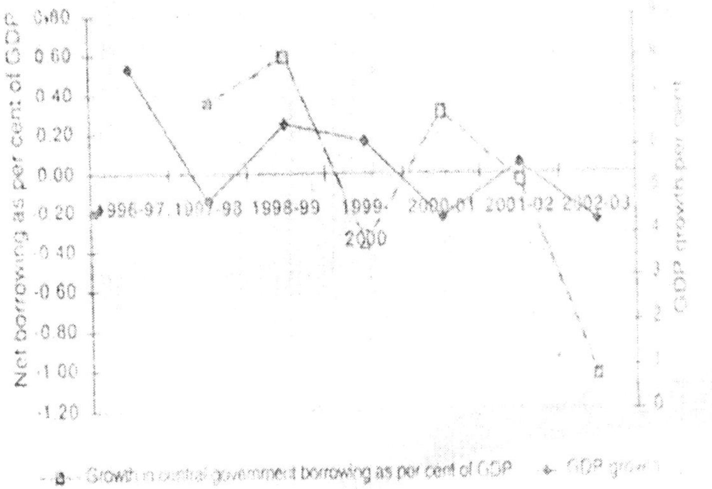

The analysis of market borrowing of 1996-97 to 2002-03 shows that the fiscal policy has been counter - cyclical in the last few years (Table A1 and Graph 10). Prior to 199-2000, it moved in tandem with GDP growth and since 1998-99 it is counter cyclical.

State government net market borrowing has been waxing and waning in tandem with GDP growth rate (Graph 11 –Growth of state governments market borrowing and GDP). A large part of state governments expenditure being pre-committed in interest payments, salary, pension etc, they have little room to alter its expenditure. Thus, state governments are obliged to meet their expenditure commitments. They tighten their belt on social and infrastructure expenditure which continues during the expansion phase of the economy as well. It may be noted that states market borrowing in the recent past may have been affected by restructuring of their debt by the RBI.

Graph 11

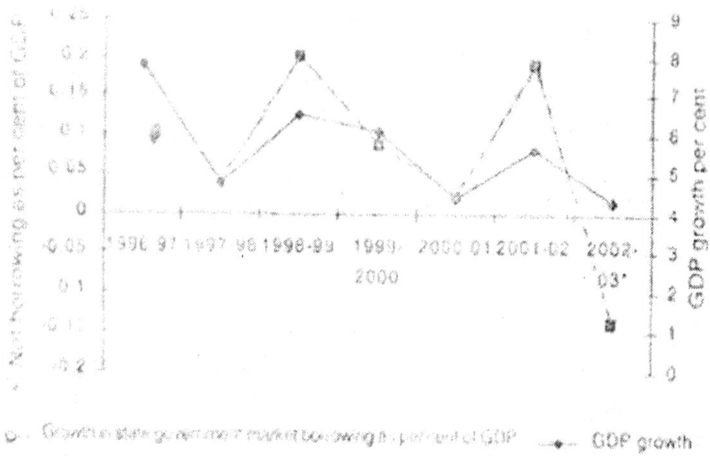

Social Expenditure and Reforms at Local Government Level

The main impact of high fiscal deficit has been short of resources to spend on social infrastructure such as education, health, water supply and sanitation. Revenue and fiscal deficit remained high and the impact of expenditure compression fell on social infrastructure (Table 4).

The ad-hoc support provided by state governments to local government has increased over the 1980s. State finance commissions which derive their authority from the 73rd and 7th Amendments recommended devolution of funds to local government. The Finance Commission (FC) based transfers have been robust to change in government, and to different parties existing at different levels of the government. This has provided some relief to social expenditure, however, there is a wide gap between their to social expenditure and their own resource base. The FC based transfer have opened possibility of securitisation of grants from states to pay for social infrastructure and not depend on the whims and fancies of state administration.

Three Scenarios

In the next few years the debt restructuring of the economy is going to have a favourable impact on government budget constraint well as fiscal deficit. A small macroeconomic model with government budget constraint built into it will be useful to predict main fiscal variables. The model can be used to forecast macroeconomic variables of the economy in short- and long-term as well. A model which takes into account impact of taxes, subsidies and other government interventions which influence the productive capacity of the economy can be effective in understanding likely unfolding scenario. A model which can predict government spending of the government.

We have used a static model to develop three scenarios business s usual, medium growth and high growth scenario based on assumptions relating to GDP growth, inflation and bank rate. Combined government receipt, expenditure and plan outlay are projected using three-year moving average rate of growth. Similarly central government fiscal variables revenue receipts, tax receipts, direct an indirect taxes, etc, have been projected. However, in government expenditure and outstanding internal debt, increase/decrease in interest outgo has been factored in.

Business–as–usual

The main assumptions in this scenario relate to GDP growth of 5.5 percent, inflation growing 4.5 percent and bank rate continues to be 5 percent p.a. Maintaining inflation rate constant satisfies the criterion of the macroeconomic stability.

Growth of combined government tax revenues which lagged behind that of government expenditure by about 0.8 percentage point will widen to 2.3 percentage point of GDP. At the combined government level. Expenditure is growing steadily because of increase in plan expenditure even though there is a gradual reduction in interest outgo. Outstanding internal debt peaks at 51.1 percent of GDP before reducing step by step as interest burden cases progressively.

Medium Growth Scenario

The main assumptions in this scenario relate to GDP growth of 7 percent annum, inflation rate growth at the rate of 4.5 percent per annum—same as that of the business–as–usual scenario. Bank rate is assumed to be 5.5 percent per anum—50 basis point more than the business-as-usual scenario.

Combined government receipt and expenditure as percentage of GDP is lower eve though in absolute money terms both are same as that of the earlier scenario. At the central government level outstanding internal debt in money terms reduce marginally but as a proportion of GDP is eight percentage points. Even though gross fiscal deficit target suggested by the EFC are not met, the outstanding internal debt is just met by 2009-10.

High Growth Scenario

The main assumptions in this scenario are average growth rate of 8 percent per annum. Inflation of 5 percent per annum 50 basis points more than the earlier scenario and bank rate of 6 percent per annum –100 basis points more than the business as usual scenario. Rationale for slightly higher rate of inflation and bank rate is that the economy may hit capacity constraint. If it grows at 8 percent annum on sustained basis. Hence, certain amount of inflationary pressure is likely to build up ad there will be some squeeze on credit availability as well.

Table 5: Macroeconomic Growth Under Business–as-usual Scenario

		2003-04	2004-05	2005-06	2006-07	2007-08	2008-09	2009-10
		Assumptions						
GDP at factor cost	% change	6.5	5.5	5.5	5.5	5.5	5.5	5.5
WPI all commodities	% change	4.5	4.5	4.5	4.5	4.5	4.5	4.5
Bank rate (March-end)	Percent	5.8	5	5	5	5	5	5
		Main fiscal variable (combined government)						
Govt. receipts	% of GDP	33.2	33.8	34.4	35.0	35.7	36.3	37.0
Govt. expenditure	% of GDP	34.0	34.7	35.6	36.5	37.4	38.3	39.3
Plan quality	% of GDP	10.2	10.6	11.0	11.5	12.0	12.4	12.9
		Central government						
Interest	% of GDP	4.5	4.3	4.1	3.9	3.7	3.6	3.4
Revenue deficit	% of GDP	4.1	4.1	4.0	3.9	3.8	3.8	3.7
Gross fiscal deficit	% of GDP	5.6	5.6	5.3	5.2	5.1	4.9	4.8
Outstanding internal debt	% of GDP	48.6	49.4	50.2	51.1	49.2	46.6	43.2

Although there is no change in combined government receipts and expenditure in absolute terms but as percentage of GDP there is approximately 5.5 percentage point change compared to the business-as-usual scenario Only under this scenario government receipts ad expenditure as percentage of GDP are lower than the base year (2003-04). There is direct impact on interest outgo as percentage of GDP and outstanding internal debt as percentage of GDP reduce by more than 14 percentage points by 2009-10. Under his scenario the internal debt forms envisaged in the EFC report (Para 3.20) are met by 2008-09, but revenue deficit norms envisaged under FRMB Act for the central government are far from the target.

Reduction in non-plan expenditures percentage of GDP, but not in nominal terms, is in agreement with the observation that increased provision to social sectors and physical infrastructure can be made only when the slide in the revenue –GDP ratio is reversed (Rao 2002).

Reduction in non-plan expenditure as percentage of GDP, but not in nominal terms, is in agreement with the observation that increased provision to social sectors and physical infrastructure can be made only when the slide in the revenue- GDP ratio is reversed (Rao 2002).

A comparative presentation (Graph 12 – Revenue deficit as percentage of GDP ad Graph 13 – Fiscal deficit as percentage of GDP) of revenue and fiscal deficit as percentage of GDP shows that the two deficits decline faster as economy grows at a faster pace. Fiscal deficit under this static model mimics changes in revenue deficit.

Graph 12: Revenue Deficit as Percentage of GDP

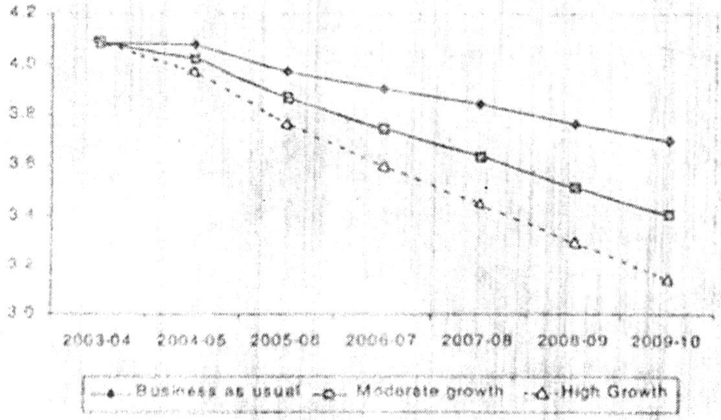

Graph 13: Fiscal Deficit as Percentage of GDP

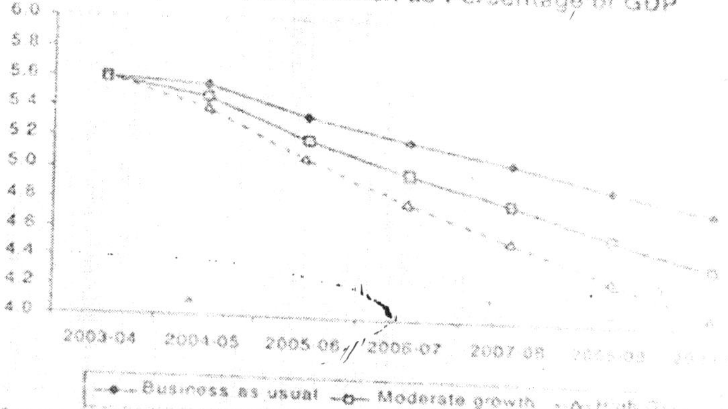

Source: Tables 5, 6 and 7

Proposals for Restructuring of Public Finances

It has been argued that the institutions of intergovernmental relations have generated perverse incentives and fiscal indiscipline among states (Anand, Bagchi and Sen 2001). The vertical imbalance which exists in Indian federal structure got further exacerbated as Indian economy opened up and increasingly depended on market based rules administered by the central bank. Before the economic reforms, the statutory institution of finance commission attempted to reduce the vertical imbalance and the horizontal disparities. It functioned well in the past as transfers were rule based and transparent. Another institution—the Planning Commission—the allocative machinery to direct savings of the economy into productive resources, also allocated resources largely based on well understood formula. The two intergovernmental institutions have continued to function in the same fashion with some minor variations but their allocations have been questioned recently as states have to attract private investment based on economic and social infrastructure available in the state. The 73rd and 74th Amendments to the Constitution have exacerbated the vertical imbalance and fiscal health of public finances. A few developments in local government finances are noteworthy and need to be highlighted s they hold promises in the future.

Table 6: Macroeconomic Growth Under Medium Growth Scenario

		2003-04	2004-05	2005-06	2006-07	2007-08	2008-09	2009-10
Assumptions								
GDP at factor cost	% change	6.5	7	7	7	7	7	7
WPI all commodities	% change	4.5	4.5	4.5	4.5	4.5	4.5	4.5
Bank rate (March-end)	Percent	5.8	5.	5.5	5.5	5.5	5.5	5.5
Main Fiscal Variable (Combined Government)								
Government receipts	% of GDP	33.2	33.3	33.5	33.6	33.8	34.0	34.1
Government expenditure	% of GDP	34.0	34.3	34.7	35.1	35.4	355.8	36.2
Plan quality	% of GDP	10.2	10.5	10.7	11.0	11.3	11.6	11.9
Central Government								
Interest	% of GDP	4.5	4.2	4.0	3.8	3.6	3.4	3.2
Revenue deficit	% of GDP	4.1	4.0	3.9	3.7	3.6	3.5	3.4
Gross fiscal deficit	% of GDP	5.6	5.5	5.2	5.0	4.8	4.6	4.4
Outstanding internal debt	% of GDP	48.6	48.2	47.7	47.0	43.6	39.7	35.2

Table 7: Macroeconomic Growth Under High Growth Scenario

		2003-04	2004-05	2005-06	2006-07	2007-08	2008-09	2009-10
Assumptions								
GDP at factor cost	% change	6.5	8	8	8	8	8	8
WPI all commodities	% change	4.5	5	5	5	5	5	5
Bank rate (March-end)	%	5.8	6	6	6	6	6	6
Main Fiscal Variable (Combined Government)								
Govt. receipts	% of GDP	33.2	32.9	32.6	32.3	32.0	31.8	31.5
Govt. expenditure	% of GDP	34.0	33.8	33.8	33.7	33.6	33.5	33.4
Plan quality	% of GDP	10.2	10.4	10.5	10.6	10.7	10.9	11.0
Central Government								
Interest	% of GDP	4.5	4.2	3.9	3.7	3.5	3.3	3.1
Revenue deficit	% of GDP	4.1	4.0	3.8	3.6	3.4	3.3	3.1
Gross fiscal deficit	% of GDP	5.6	5.4	5.1	4.8	4.6	4.3	4.1
Outstanding internal debt	% of GDP	48.6	47.1	45.3	43.3	38.8	33.9	28.8

3

Reforms in Transfers to States

In India, transfer from the center to states constitutes a large proportion of Planning Commission transfers. Plan/non-plan distinction is non-operational. Linkage between loan disbursement from the Planning Commission or capital projects and actual spending on capital projects is weak.

Capital expenditure under plan and non-plan given rise to step-motherly treatment to the maintenance of physical assets created under plan heads. In the coming years as states are expected to raise part of the resources from the capital market, it should be left to the market to assess viability of economic infrastructure projects. Social infrastructure and maintenance which bears the burden of cuts in revenue expenditure may benefit form abolition of artificial distinction between plan and non-plan expenditure. Rethinking on institutional role of the state planning bodies and the central planning Commission needs to be undertaken when allocations of resources are guided by markets.

Prior to the implementation of MTFRP, states had an incentive to launch new programmes to qualify for loan and grant financing under their respective state plan for the first few years, after that they get transferred to non-plan account and, thus, required to be supported by general purpose grants form the centre or their own resources (McCarten 2003). The coordination between state plans and Finance Commission transfers has began since 2002-03.

Traditionally, projects and schemes meant for states were used to be location-specific or project-specific. To finance planned projects, financial resources were available to states form state owned controlled financial institutions and the institutions assumed that the due diligence has been done by the Planning Commission. This method suited nationwide plan allocations carried out by the Central Planning Commission. The fall-out of this methodology under a market based allocation system produced structural infirmities which have been addressed by the RBI and the central government (RBI 2002 and 2003c). The new trend in transfers from center to states is that they are becoming increasingly sector-specific and are based on reform conditionalities (output performance). As a result total transfer to states may be able to balance redistribute demand of states without being regressive. For example, APDRP and Urban Reform Incentive Fund are sectoral initiatives and outside the Gadgil formula. Hence, the role of the Planning Commission and state plans needs to be considered carefully in the emerging scenario. Reform conditionalities must be crafted carefully. For example, under the States, Fiscal Reform Facility, now part of MTFRP of most of the states, targets are same for all states having revenue deficits. These targets fro fiscally better off states is stiffer than worse off states. The finance Commission should recommend a trajectory for reduction in revenue deficit so that efforts made by states commensurate with the incentive provided to them from the facility.

Devolution as a Proportion of Tax Receipts or Fixed Sum

In order to raise accountability and to contain fiscal imbalances, the intergovernmental transfers could be broadly dived into specific purpose and general purpose grants. General purpose grants have been allocated as proportion of revenue collected by the center using a pre-determined formula suggested by the Finance Commission.

When the economy has not been functioning at full employment level, revenue collections fall and these transfers in absolute terms shrink and result in higher revenue deficit of state governments. Further , the management of cash flows at state level becomes difficult, given the nature of transfers. The state finance secretaries generally agree that two of the major factors contributing to liquidity problems, even after discounting the adverse impact of the deficit are: *(i)* the abrupt shortfalls in actual monthly transfers from the central government to the states as compared to the budget estimates and *(ii)* the bunching of releases of plan funds for the central sector and centrally-sponsored schemes especially in the last quarter of the financial year. The latter, generally released in the last quarter, exacerbate liquidity problem as expenditure is incurred uniformly throughout the year (RBI 2003c).

Moving from general purpose grants to specific purpose grants is going to worsen this further as tied grants strap the hands of the recipient states. The states have also complained that a larger share of plan finances is given as earmarked funds on centrally sponsored schemes, that too outside the consolidated fund of the state, and that only a smaller share is being received as untied plan loans (RBI 2003c). This view is in line with the observations that states have often expressed a preference for tax devolution because of in-built buoyancy in tax receipts (Sen 2000). This is true when economy is growing at a higher clip, but reverse happens during economic downturn.

The method of transfer is an issue which needs to be addressed. Given the similarities in fiscal structure of India and Australia, we should take a leaf from their book. Enforcing a hard budget constraint is probably not a feasible solution for India at this stage of economic development and of bond market (see box). A middle way is that transfers are divided into two parts. First is a fixed part which is in line with the committed revenue expenditure of the state, i.e. expenditure on social infrastructure and interest. And second part of transfer is project specific which is disbursed in line with the conditionalities placed on these transfers with or without incentives.

The sector specific transfers based on output-based rather than input-based measures can be best illustrated from the AIBP and APDRAP. The AIBP which is project specific but without any output based performance measure has shown no visible result. Irrigation subsidies are unlikely to show any improvement in the near future. The unholy nexus between cooperative banks and irrigation development corporations needs a high level of political commitment to crack. A debt restructuring programme on the lines of one time settlement of SEB dues at individual state level is required to ease burden on state government budgets without having an unfavourable fall out form cooperative bank depositors.

On the other hand, APDRP which is sector specific with output based performance measures has started showing reduction in cash losses. Moreover, the performance base fiscal transfers recommended by the Finance Commission could set an example for state finance commissions for transfers to local government bodies. Such targeting would ensure that wherever user charges have to be levied, they must believed and must be monitored . The finance Commission decision in this regard can help targeting of social expenditure. Under this method, a certain proportion of transfers will be progressive and improve efficiency of resources.

Implementation of VAT

Apart from reforming the transfer system, it is important to plug the vertical gap by assignment of tax powers to states. This would reduce the burden placed on the transfer system. It is generally accepted that the competition among states to give incentives for industrialization has only resulted in a race to the bottom. To attract industries, states provided multiyear sales tax exemptions to industries. One of the reasons for states inability to improve their own-tax collection as percentage of GDP is that they have already mortgaged future tax revenues. With the 89th Amendment of the Constitution, the revenue form the central tax on services is also becoming available for sharing of form and services have been allowed to be taxed by states as well with the production and consumption of services coming within the tax et the buoyancy in states taxes as well as expansion of tax base will get improved as states will be able to levy VAT on services.

Table A1: Market Borrowings and Coupon Rates on Central Government Dated Securities

Fiscal year	Outstanding dated Securities (Rs Cr)	Conversion of Ad hoc treasury Bills (Rs Cr)	Total outstanding (Rs Cr)	Weighted average yield (%)	Growth of central govt. debt as % of GDP	GDP growth	GDP (Rs Cr)
1996-97	6666	121818	128484	13.69		7.8	1368200
1997-98	1977	101818	133795	12.01	0.35	4.8	1522500
1998-99	42212	101818	144030	11.86	0.59	6.5	1740900
1999-00	35190	101818	137008	11.77	-0.36	6.1	1933700
2000-01	41732	101818	143550	10.95	0.31	4.4	2104300
2001-02	40927	101818	142745	9.44	-0.04	5.6	2296000
2002-03	55438	61818	117256	7.34	-1.03	4.3	2472800
2003-04	83574	41818	125392	5.94			

Table A2: Repayment Schedule for Market Loans of Central Governments

Fiscal year	Amount of Repayment (Rs. Crore)	GDP in line with Business as usual scenario	Percent of GDP
2003-04	32910		
2004-05	34316		
2005-06	35631	2744800	1.20
2006-07	36894	3019279	1.14
2007-08	41151	3321207	1.07
2008-09	40223	3653328	1.01
2009-10	45195	4018660	1.02
2010-11	53109	4420526	0.91
2011-12	45610	4862579	0.93
2012-13	46255		
2013-14	40191		

2014-15	27588
2015-16	36857
2016-17	36130
2017-18	37000
2018-19	16632
2019-20	11000
2020-21	11000
2021-22	13213
2022-23	13000
2026-27	15000
2032-33	5000

Table A3: Interest Rate Profile of Outstanding Central Government Securities

Amount of Repayment (Rs. Crore)	*GDP in line with Business as usual scenario*	*Percent of GDP*
5.03-5.99	12378	1.84
6.00-6.99	44684	6.63
7.00-7.99	79654	11.82
8.00-8.99	29643	4.40
9.00-9.99	51992	7.72
10.00-10.99	84572	12.55
11.00-11.99	212243	31.49
12.00-12.99	125047	18.56
13.00-13.99	33692	5.00
Total	673905	

Source: RBI (2003b)

The introduction of destination based VAT in all the states, is an important reform. Compared to present indirect tax system at the centre and states. VAR is a simple, transparent and rule based tax system. In addition to changing the overall structure of commodity taxes in the country, the implementation will have a direct impact on widening the tax base for the centre as well as states. The management information system required to implement the VAT successfully in the country would make tax avoidance difficult and thee is an in built incentive for tax compliance . it will be beneficial for the government as well as for honest tax payers. In India, like other federal governments, would face difficulty in harmonizing tax on interstate trade while implementing VAT but these complexities are not insurmountable (purohit 2002).

Table A5: Strategic Sale of PSEs Year 2000 Onwards

Sr No	Name of PSE	Date	Ratio of Paid up Equity Sold (Per Cent)	Face Value of Equity Sold (Rs in Crore)	Realisation (Rs Crores)
1	Modern Foods	Jan-00	74	9.63	105
			26	3.38	44
2	LJMC	Jul-00	74	6.?	2.53
3	BALCO ^	Mar-01	51	112.52	826.5
4	CMC	Oct-01	51	7.73	152
5	HTL	Oct-01	74	11.1	55
6	VSNL ^	Feb-02	25	71.2	3,689
7	IBP	Feb-02	33.6	7.4	1,153.70
8	PPL	Feb-02	74	320.1	151.7
9	Jessop*	Feb-02	72	68.1	18.2
10	HZL	Apr-02	26	109.8	445
11	IPCL	May-02	26	64.5	1,490.80
12	Maruti Udyog	May-02	27.5	39.73	1,993
13	ICVL**	Apr-03	51	6.21	16
14-16	HCI	2001-02			
	(3 hotels)	various dates	100	14.7	242.5
17-35	ITDC	2001-02			
	(19 hotels)	various dates	100	27.1	444.1
Total				900.17	11,260.23

Notes: ^ Including dividend and Divi. T[illegible] of surplus cash [illegible] to disinvestment.
* Subject to court order. ** Subject to [illegible] approval.
Source: www.disinvest.[illegible]

The transition to a VAT system in India has not come about due to expected loss in revenue, administrative difficulties without much computerization, resistance from tax payers and the problem of border adjustment in place of the central sales tax (Purohit 2001). Nevertheless, VAT is growing in importance as a national tax around the world and at the sub-national level.

The main reason is that user charges and property tax usually preferred for financing local governments are difficult to implement and are not able to fill the fiscal gap where major spending responsibilities of local governments are in social areas such as drinking water, health and education (Bird 2000).

It is disheartening that broad-based tax reforms have not kept pace with liberalization in financial markets, banking sector and goods market. Restructuring of indirect finances, especially, implementation of VAT in the country can expand the tax base further. An expanding tax base in the medium term at the state and local government level would reduce the burden placed on federal transfer to provide resources to meet expenditure needs of the social as well as economic sectors.

Table A6: Status of Investment in State Level Public Enterprise (March 31, 2001)

Name of the state	*Approx No. of state level public enterprises (SLEPs)*	*Estimated Total investment in SLPEs (Rs. In crore)*	*Net accumulated Loss (Rs. In crore)*	*Approx no. of loss making SLPEs*	*Approx no. of non working SLPEs*
Andhra Pradesh	128	48794	2919	62	9
Assam	42	3649	2792	28	10
Delhi	N/A	N/A	N/A	N/A	N/A
Goa	12	4869	730	N/A	N/A
Gujarat	54	23438	965	N/A	N/A
Haryana	45	443	384	10	4
Himachalpradesh	21	3143	369	12	2
Jammu Kashmir	N/A	N/A	N/A	N/A	N/A
Karnataka	76	19295	811	37	13
Kerala	109	9805	1124	52	13
Madhya Pradesh	26	7923	600	8	15
Maharashtra	65	22477	N/A	28	17
Manipur	14	N/A	N/A	10	N/A
Orissa	68	9796	1180	18	34
Punjab	53	12425	847	25	23
Rajasthan	24	11576	261	6	3
Tamilnadu	59	6192	N/A	33	12
Uttar pradesh	41	17773	5327	21	19
West Bengal	82	18241	5068	59	6
Total	919	219839	23377	409	180

N/A: Not available

Source: State government. IPE Hyderabad and other sources

Table A7: Disinvestments in States

Name of the state	*Approx No. of state level public enterprises (SLEPs)*	*SLPEs identified for Disin-vestment. Winding up/restru-cturing*	*No. of SLPEs in which process initiated*	*No. of SLPEs privatized*	*No. of SLPEs non closed Down*
AndhraPradesh	128	87	7.9	12	12
Assam	42	N/A	N/A	-	-
Delhi	N/A	N/A	1	1	-
Goa	12	2	2	2^	-
Gujarat	54	24	24	1	6
Haryana	45	22	13	1	12
Himachalpradesh	21	15	5	3	2
Jammukashmir	N/A	7	2	-	2
Karnataka	76	20	20	2	11
Kerala	109	12	-	-	-
Madhya Pradesh	26	14	14	1	-
Maharashtra	65	6	4	-	-
Manipur	14	10	N/A	-	-
Orissa	68	27	27	8	11
Punjab	53	10	10		5
Rajasthan	24	10	6	1	1
Tamilnadu	59	13	3	-	12
Uttar pradesh	41	9	9	-	-
West Bengal	82	290	2	1#	-
Total	919		221	33	69

Table A8: Market Borrowings and Coupon Rates On State Government Dated Securities

Fiscal year	*Net market borrowing (Rs crore)*	*Weighted coupon/cut-off yield (percent)*	*Growth in state governments debt as % of GDP*	*GDP growth*
1996-97	6536	13.83		7.8
1997-98	7193	12.82	0.043	4.8
1998-99	10700	12.35	0.201	6.5
1999-2000	12405	11.89	0.088	6.1
2000-01	12880	10.99	0.023	4.4
2001-02	17261	9.2	0.191	5.6
2002-03	13874	7049	-0.137	4.3

Table A9: Repayment Schedule For Market Loans of State Governments

Fiscal year	*Amount of Repayment (Rs. Crore)*	*GDP in line with Business as usual scenario*	*Percent of GDP*
2003-04	4145	2744800	0.15
2004-05	5123	3019279	0.17
2005-06	6274	3321207	0.19
2006-07	6551	3653328	0.18
2007-08	11554	4018660	0.29
2008-09	14400	4420526	0.33
2009-10	16511	4862579	0.34
2010-11	15870		
2011-12	22032		
2012-13	20065		

Table A10: Interest Rate Profile of Outstanding State Government Loans

Range of interest rate (percent)	*Outstanding (Rs crore)*	*Percent of total*
<7	19585	14.72
7.00-7.99	11030	8.29
8.00-8.99	8004	6.02

9.00-9.99	5411	4.07
10.00-10.99	14563	10.94
11.00-11.99	17062	12.82
12.00-12.99	31269	23.50
13.00 and >	26142	19.65
Total	133066	

Conclusion

The Eleventh Finance Commission (EFC) had recommended restructuring of government finances which would usher macro economic stability by 2004-05. The commission emphasized that revenue deficit must be reduced at an accelerated pace to reduce fiscal deficit and to make resources available for social infrastructure. At full employment level there should be surplus on revenue account and stock of debt should be around 55 percent of GDP. In the past few years restructuring of debt domestic as well as foreign has gained momentum. There is a distinct shift in refinancing of high cost debt which is going to reduce revenue deficit as proportion of GDP in the coming years. Inflation is under control and the central bank has taken advantage of the development to reduce bank rates signaling reduction in internal rates on savings contractual as well as voluntary one which underpinned market interest rates.

Liberalization of economic markets and strengthening of feral structure of India has made the environment ripe for more institutional reforms including strengthening of hard budget constraints, especially, for states. Implementation of FRBM and MTFRP, restructuring of debt, introduction of user pays principle for power and sector specific conditional loans and grants to states would show results in medium term. Subsidies related to irrigation development schemes still remain a knotty problem in some states. However, the debt obligations for most states under MTFRP are manageable in medium term and should help states in controlling their fiscal deficits.

Revenue and fiscal deficits have remained stubbornly high. Our analysis shows that the high level of debt would continue to plague revenue deficit and would only case gradually by 2010 unless there is a spurt in economic growth on a sustained basis. Consistent economic growth rate of 8 percent per year which would make the economy grow at its full employment level would see the deficit targets as well as expenditure level being met in medium term.

With the production and consumption of services coming within the tax net, the buoyancy in states taxes as well as enhancement of tax base will get improved as they will be able to levy VAT on services. The in-built fiscal gap between center and states has placed enormous pressure on federal transfers. Assignment of taxation power is one area, especially through VAT on services, that will help in filling the gap partly.

Capital expenditure under plan and non-plan has given rise to the neglect of maintenance of physical assets created under plan heads. Although, central government expenditure seems to be counter cyclical, it has not helped states. So far during economic downturn lower revenue transfers to states have exacerbated their revenue deficits and capacity to spend on social infrastructure. Social infrastructure and maintenance which bear the burden of cuts in revenue expenditure may benefit from abolition of artificial distinction between plan and non plan expenditure. Rethinking on institutional role of the state planning bodies and the central Planning commission needs to be under taken when allocations of resources are guided by markets. Transfer to states partly as fixed sum and the rest linked to specific programme / project with or without incentive payment can ameliorate the cascading effect of lower than anticipated revenue collection. Thee is a need to break the nexus between state governments revenue deficit with that of the central government by making committed expenditure on social infrastructure free from economic growth cycle. Incentive based transfer to sector specific and project specific is required to improve productivity of capital expenditure.

Legislative and administrative changes required to contain revenue and fiscal deficits are in place. Its implementation in medium term, assuming continuation of favourable macro economic scenario moderate interest and inflation rates will reduce the deficits. Now, the main issues I restructuring of public finances are implementation of VAT, rethinking on the role of intergovernmental institutions responsible for allocation of resources and mechanism of transfer to states for their capital expenditure.

4

Impact of VAT on Central and State Finance

Introduction

After 1994 report on the reform of domestic trade taxes in India, there was not much action in planning for a change in regime from a predominantly first–point sales tax to a value added tax (VAT) system as proposed in the report. In 1998. Madhya Pradesh proposed to latterly introduce VAT and initiated the process of preparing fir it. While the preparations were still on, same landmark decisions were made at the national level. On November 19, 1999, in a meeting with the union finance minister, the state chief ministers decided to adhere to some floor rate for an agreed set of commodities, withdraw various schemes for tax-based incentives to industry for new investments, and jointly introduce VAT. The first two measures were to take effect from January 1, 2000, and VAT was to be introduce from April 1, 2000. The deadline for the first two measured was met but the third step has faced a number of rescheduled deadline ad now stands postponed without a deadline.

The move to introduce floor rates was aimed stemming tax competition among states, which it was felt resulted in therein of the tax base of all the states. Tax competition included competition in rates as well as in providing tax-based industrial incentives, where the basis for providing incentives was getting progressively watered down while the extent of incentives provided tended to get more liberal. While no individual state had an incentive to unilaterally change this regime, there were perceptible benefits from joint withdrawal of these incentives, in the form of higher revenue realizations. This became the basis for the agreement on a joint withdrawal from a regime of tax competition by all the state.

The scenario changes somewhat in the context of introduction of VAT. From the state government's point of view, the benefits of introducing VAT in place of the present sale tax result from extending the tax base to cover transactions hitherto not subject to a levy. The costs associated with a transition are concerned with providing set-off for input taxes and zero rating interstate trade and exports. While the former tend to be unknown quantities, the latter become the visible losses to the exchequer. Further, since the content of economic activity varies across sates and along with it the composition of tax collected also varies, the net benefit from introducing VAT can vary significantly across states. Apprehensions on the dimensionality of gain/loss possibly created some discomfort among the states, while uncertainly in the nature of changes in the forms of administration stirred resistance from the dealers. This paper looks at the first issue in a bid address at least part of the problem.

Section II attempts to detail the impact on state finances for major states in the country. Given the sensitivity of the states to potential loss of revenue from the changeover, the finance minister has provided an assurance of compensation for loss of revenue, if any. This section therefore also presents an analysis of the likely impact on central finances of such an assurance.

The proposed shift in regime is also being projected as the right time to ensure convergence in the tax structures and tax rates. While the empowered committee of state finance ministers decided on the desirability of uniform rates of tax on a well defined set of commodities as an integral part of the VAT design the central government put forward the need for greater convergence in the entire structure of the law and rules. The implications of this emphasis on greater convergence, if not complete homogeneity for central and state finances are taken up in Section III. Section IV provides some concluding observations.

Estimates of Impact of VAT

This exercise seeks to assess the change in tax revenue that could result from the introduction of VAT by all states, following a uniform design. The key features of such design would be tax credit for inputs, extension of the base to include transactions beyond the first-point sale and zero-rating of interstate trade and international exports. The tax rates proposed are 4 percent and 12.5 percent, with the former rate being applicable mainly on inputs and some basic necessities. The tax would, however, remain a tax on sale of goods alone.

It should be pointed out that a VAT with these features would not provide all the textbook benefits of the introduction of VAT. Exclusion of services from the base, eve if the states are empowered to tax selected services on a standalone basis, would not eliminate the problem of cascading form the tax system. Services here would be like exempt goods, and exemption within a VAT regime brings back the problem of cascading. As a result, the tax would not be a completely transparent one. This move should therefore be considered only as a step in the transition to a complete VAT that includes goods and services.

In order to assess the impact of VAT on central and state revenues the following methodology was adopted. Since it is generally recognized that the major part of the tax base of any state within sales tax manufacturing sector output, with organized manufacturing contributing the major share, the present exercise limits itself to exploring the impact taking the registered manufacturing sector s the base. It makes use of manufacturing sector data level of classification, the input output tables and data on sales tax collections of individual states, decomposed into general sales tax levied on local sales and central sales tax levied on interstate sales.

The ASI provides data on total inputs as well as total output of industry groups. Since the inputs here include both taxed inputs as well as exempt inputs, an attempt is made to first segregate the taxed inputs and allow for tax credit for the same. To identify the taxed inputs, the 1993-94 input-output table is used. The input-output table was reconstructed/collapsed to achieve a correspondence with the ASI two digit classification for the manufacturing sector. Since the taxed inputs are mainly from the manufacturing sector, the share of manufacturing sector inputs to total inputs (Excluding service sector inputs as well as electricity, gas and water supply), is use as a proxy for the proportion of taxed inputs total material inputs. Further, since a part of the inputs s procedure form outside the state, the tax credit in any give state would only be to the extent to taxable inputs procedure in that state. For the purposes of this exercise it is assumed that 50 percent of the inputs are locally procured and the rest are procured through interstate transactions. Thus, applying these two ratios to the vale of material inputs for each industry group and using 4 percent as the rate of tax on all inputs, yields the amount of loss in revenue on account of tax rebate.

The above process should result in decline in the cost of inputs to the manufacturing sector. If the entire cost of the tax was hitherto being passed on as lower value of outputs. The value of output, therefore, is correspondingly adjusted downwards. Following from this lower value of output, the tax on output too would be lower. The reduction of tax collection on this count is computed assuming 4 percent rate of tax.

Since the tax base is expected to include second and subsequent sales as well as , an increase in tax collections is anticipated on this account. Here, three alternative assumptions on increments to value added are considered 20,15 and 20 percent over the value of output from manufacturing. The ratio of value added in trade to that in manufacturing is over 100 percent. Assuming that trade is associated with all goods activities, that is with agriculture as well as manufacturing, the prorated ratio for manufacturing would be 45 percent, which continues to be higher than he proportions assumed in the present exercise. Similarly, for products sold with a printed MRp price, the Central Excise department has adopted drawback rates related to MRP. These rates range between 30 and 50 percent, a large segment of the commodities being offered 35 percent or 40 percent rates. The latter would translate into 54 and 67 percent value added over the assigned cost of manufacture. These figures once again seem to suggest that the adopted increments to value added of 10,15 and 20 percent are underestimates. The rationale for these rates, however, is derived from the fact that the existing sales tax regimes are not taxes on manufacturing alone, but on the first sales in the state, a base, which includes goods brought into the state by way of interstate sales. The latter set of transactions tends to capture a part of the value added in trade Further, discussion with officials of the sales tax departments in various state suggest that the perception is one of relatively low feasible increments to value added. Therefore, in order to provide conservative estimates of increments to tax collections the present exercise considers only the above in increments to value added.

Since the consensus s far has been on 12.5 percent being the VAT rate, the exceptions largely being inputs which are to be taxed at 4 percent, this exercise assumes that the above increments to value added do get taxed at 12.5 percent.

Zero-rating of interstate trade too would result in a decline in revenues to the state. Assuming that interstate sale from any state is only of goods manufactured in that state, zero –rating of interstate trade would mean loss of the present collections of CST revenue. This provides an estimate of the loss of revenue from zero-rating of interstate trade of goods. An aggregating of these three components on the impact of introduction of VAT at the national level is presented in Table 1. From the table, it appears that aggregating over all states. VAT would yield net additional revenue provided there is more that 15 percent value addition in goods beyond the manufacturing stage.

Netimpact=0.125*α*(VO-VI*β*.04)-VI*β*.04* (0.5+0.04)-CST =0.15*α* VO-CST-VI*β*.04*(0.125*α+0.54)

Where VO is the value of output, VI is value of inputs, α is the proportion by which value increased in the second and subsequent sales and β is the ratio of taxed inputs to total inputs.

The results are reported in Table 1 and include three scenarios:

- *Case 1:* full VT on goods including sugar, textiles and tobacco, with full credit for capital goods:
- *Case 2:* VAT on goods excluding sugar, textiles and tobacco;
- *Case 3:* VAT on all goods without credit for capital goods.

This is a picture that has been aggregated over all states. The impact, however, would very considerably across states depending on the relation between local production and consumption. For instance, a state with very little manufacturing activity would find very little loss of revenue from input tax credit for the manufacturing sector. N the other had, states with large manufacturing bases are likely to face higher costs on the count. Aggregating over all the state stands to glass over these differences, which would acquire a lot of importance in the context of a central government decision to financially support the shift to a VAT regime.

An attempt is made below to identify the man statewise effects. The exercise is limited to exploring the effects within Case 1 above, and can be replicated for the other cases as well as. As in the aggregate analysis, the effects are classified into four parts loss from providing input tax credit, loss from reduced value of output, loss from removal of CST and gains from taxing second and subsequent sales within the state.

(1) *Loss from providing input-tax credit:* Taking the industry group-based figures for loss from tax credit, and the share of individual states in the particular industry, one can derive the total cost from providing tax credit. However, give the assumption that only 50 percent of the inputs used in a state are locally purchased, the loss to the state exchequer would be half of the total cost thus estimated.

Table 1: Gain/Loss from a Switchover to VT

Value Added	*10 percent*	*15 percent*	*20 percent*
Case 1	-5480	-1122	3235
Case 2	-5126	-1441	2244
Case 3	-4052	319	4691

2. *Loss front reduced value of output:* Assuring that lower costs in the form of tax credit are passed on to buyers through lower prices, the value of output would be lower by the full amount of tax on inputs. The loss to the exchequer therefore would be 4 percent of has amount.

3. *Loss from removal of CST:* The loss on this count is straight forward—the entire revenue from CST as n the date of with drawal of CST.

4. Gain from taxation of second and subsequent sales in the state. Three scenarios re considered –10 percent. 15 percent and 20 percent increase in value added. Allocating this value added across states, however, is not straightforward, since goods

manufactured in a state are not necessarily trade are not available. Destination based numbers for interstate trade are not available, therefore, the only other alternative is to look at consumption numbers as reflected in NSS data. Taking NSS data for non agricultural consumption, shared in consumption for all the states were work out and data used as a basis to allocate the incremental value added.

Table 2 summarizes these numbers. Comparing the figures in Tables 1 and 2, while 20 percent value addition in case 1 in Table 1 suggests increases in aggregate tax collections, Table 2 indicates that the increase may not be manifest in all states. Gujarat, Haryana, Maharshtra and Tamilnadu emerge as states likely to experience some decline in revenue collections. With only 10 percent increase in value added. Andhra Pradesh, Bihar, Karnataka Madhya Pradesh and West Bengal join the states with decline in tax collections. Table 3 presents the corresponding costs of compensation for 1997-98. Assuming that the proportion of loss total sales tax revenue of the states remains unchanged over time, the loss is projected for subsequent years and compared with central tax revenue receipts, net of states' share. Depending on the assumptions regarding increments to value added, the compensation to be provided to the states varies between 1.53 percent an 5.15 percent.

This exercise does not take certain features of the economy into account.

- Zero rating of exports—Exports from state contain two components; exports to other states an those outside the country. The former is associated with central sales tax in the existing

Table 2: Impact of Introduction of VAT
(Rs crore)

	Loss Due to			Gain Due to Tax on VA			Net Impact (1997-98)		
	Tax Credit	Reduction in Value of Output	CST Withdrawal	20 Per Cent	15 Per Cent	10 Per Cent	20 Per Cent	15 Per Cent	10 Per Cent
Andhra Pradesh	384.14	15.37	623.24	1628	1221	814	605	198	-209
Assam	47.13	1.89	0	277	208	139	228	159	89
Bihar	248.15	9.93	353.66	881	661	440	269	49	-171
Gujarat	851.91	34.08	677.93	954	716	477	-610	-848	-1087
Haryana	261.11	10.44	491.65	426	320	213	-65	-172	-279
Himachal Pradesh	30.81	1.23	21.85	99	74	50	77	53	28
J and K	7.63	0.31	0	143	107	71	135	99	63
Karnataka	312.45	12.50	213.17	854	641	427	316	102	-111
Kerala	174.55	6.98	163.13	820	615	410	475	270	65
Madhya Pradesh	320.20	12.81	432.42	1128	846	564	362	80	-202
Maharashtra	1395.90	55.84	1278.28	2235	1676	1118	-495	-1054	-1612
Orissa	93.01	3.72	0	295	221	148	199	125	51
Punjab	228.71	9.15	270.31	588	441	294	311	164	17
Rajasthan	204.87	8.19	115.17	788	591	394	460	263	66
Tamil Nadu	611.81	24.47	1034.58	1543	1157	772	-128	-514	-899
Uttar Pradesh	532.94	21.32	237.06	2298	1724	1149	1507	932	358
West Bengal	274.27	10.97	332.09	1170	878	585	553	260	-32
Delhi	116.97	4.68	0	718	539	359	718	539	359

Notes: 1 The figures for CST collections are taken from RBI. For 1997-98, a few states have reported zero collections. If this is a result of incorrect accounting, the loss from introduction of VAT in these states would be higher.

2 Delhi, Haryana, Himachal Pradesh and Punjab have modified versions of last point taxation, which eliminates input taxation in the existing regime. Therefore, these costs would not exist for these states. However, the gain to revenue is assumed to accrue since the present structure of taxes is recognised to result in tax leakage.

regime. Correction for which is already made in the present exercise. The latter set of sales, however, is not associated with any tax. Data on state-wise exports too are not readily available. Hence this feature could not be incorporated into the exercise incorporating its impact would increase the losses.

- Some states have turnover taxes on second and subsequent sales. The increments to revenue form taxation of second and subsequent sales in such states would be smaller. The data on tax collections against such provisions are however not readily available and hence the corrections could not be attempted.
- Introduction of VAT as well as withdrawal of CST can alter the structure, and more importantly, the locational choice of business/industry. Some

of these changes can have an impact on revenues in the new regime. Existing sales tax regimes are argued to promote vertical integration, resulting in some inefficiencies I production. Introduction of VAT can therefore be see as promoting vertical disintegration/specialization, thereby improving efficiency, production and hence taxes due on the same. Similarly, withdrawal of CST can introduce a change in locational preferences of agents. This component, however, is not expected to change the allocation of revenues across states once the sates adopt a destination based VAT, since the taxes due to a state would be related to the consumption base in the state and not the production base. This exercise assumes that the structure remains stable.

Table 3: Projected Impact

(Rs crore)

	1997-98	1998-99	1999-2000	2000-01	2001-02 (RE)	2002-03 (BE)
Sales tax collections	48842	53116	62301	73364	79805	90496
Central tax collections (net)	95672	104652	128271	136659	142348	172964
Loss (20 per cent)	1424	1549	1816	2139	2327	2638
Loss/central taxes (per cent)	1.49	1.48	1.42	1.57	1.63	1.53
Loss (15 per cent)	2715	2953	3463	4078	4436	5030
Loss/central taxes (per cent)	2.84	2.82	2.70	2.98	3.12	2.91
Loss (10 per cent)	4808	5229	6133	7222	7858	8908
Loss/central taxes (per cent)	5.03	5.00	4.78	5.28	5.52	5.15

powers to the states is meant to provide them autonomy in determining the desirable/suitable structure of taxes along with a package of services tailored to local needs and demands. He need for autonomy is well understood and extensively written about. Differences in the composition of economic activity, differences in climatic patterns as well as income levels of states could pose differing demands on the government for provision of public or merit goods. Smaller size of market—either in terms of dispersed populations or law levels of income—would require roads as a public good; with high concentration of population and enhanced economic activity, the same can be sustained through private provision. The prioritization of publicly provided services by the local population can therefore very across states.

On the other hand, local perception of the suitability

of a state government as the appropriate service provider too may vary. Small ,dispersed communities may want to assign a smaller role for a pan-state government, give the relatively infrequent interactions with he state government; consider the tribal populations in Madhya Pradesh/Chhattisgarh/Jharkhand or the small habitations of desert Rajasthan. The same at varying levels can be true for different states with varying levels of income, and/or different levels of integration/ monetisation of the economies. This would get reflected in the state's relatively poorer ability to collect taxes, causing variations in the tax–to–GSDP ratio across states. Table 4 presents a comparison of the own tax revenue to GSDP ratios as well s sales tax collections to GSDP for major states. AS is evident from the table, there is considerable variation in the ratios across state. This ratio is not directly related to per capita income alone. Kerala and Tamil Nadu record the highest ratios for sales tax, while their rank in terms of per capital income is considerably lower, as also in the size of the secondary sector.

The comparison seems to be a reflection not only of differences in the size of the tax base of states but also in their rates and in their ability to collect taxes. Treating this as a reflection of differences I in the demands placed by the constituents of the state for government-financed public services and goods, it can be argued that the states do utilize their autonomy to appropriately customize the package of taxes and services to local preferences. In other words, the states do value their autonomy. Homogeneity in terms of structure and rates of tax would mean a loss of autonomy with direct implications in terms of reduced flexibility.

The call for homogeneity stems firm two related

arguments one, homogeneity would reduce the scope for tax competition among states, a process which tends to corrode the tax base. The argument here is fairly straightforward: tax competition n terms of rate wars and tax-based industrial incentives introduce as element of tailspin. Any measure initiated by any state would be mimicked by other s, resulting not so much in changes in patterns of investment as desired, but rather in the tax collection. Huts, homogeneity would introduce and element of stability into the tax system, allowing tax departments as well as manufacturers/traders to focus on their primary activity. While the impact of this is difficult to capture, the differentials in the tax GSDP ratios across states suggest that ax competition does not succeed in eliminating all differences in rates and structures across state Karnataka and Tamilnadu, for instance, levy and collect some turnover taxes beyond the first sale as well, which is not replicated by other states. Delhi, Punjab, Haryna and Himachal Pradesh provide differing degrees of set-off for inputs purchased by manufacturers, while other states collect 2-4 percent tax on purchases by manufactures. These differentials have not vanished over time, suggesting that the states do maintain some elements of differences although convergence In the rates is evidence in the case highly mobile goods such as motor cars and computers.

Table 4: Tax GDP Ratio

	Own tax revenue	*Sales tax revenue*	*Per capita income (Rs)*	*Share of secondary sector*
Andhra Pradesh	7.28	4.99	10591	22.85
Assam	4.33	2.62	6813	19.45
Bihar	5.05	3.16	5134	21.12
Gujarat	7.67	4.82	15636	39.22

Haryana	7.29	4.08	15747	29.86
Karnataka	8.15	4.93	12291	26.32
Kerala	8.01	5.95	11286	22.12
Madhya Pradesh	5.83	2.57	8678	24.85
Maharashtra	7.15	4.35	17252	31.48
Orissa	4.70	3.05	6293	18.38
Punjab	6.30	3.15	16947	23.97
Rajasthan	6.04	3.23	9334	26.59
Tamil Nadu	8.57	5.51	13912	32.36
Uttar Pradesh	5.01	2.72	7149	25.72
West Bengal	3.83	2.57	10388	19.59

Note: The data pertains to 1999-2000.

Second, state specific tax systems with central sales tax in its present form result in the formation of small protected markets for each state. CST in its present form serves as a protective barrier against goods flowing into the state, although it is collected and retained by the exporting state. This sustains input taxation and a corresponding rate within the state. These processes together encourage vertical integration within a state as a means of reducing the incidence of tax. On the other hand, it could also encourage duplication of economic activity across states, given the CST induced costs. In other words, the tax system would not be neutral to economic activity. For the integration of the domestic market into one integrated market, uniformity in structures and rates as well as elimination of CST in its present form would be desirable. This could offer benefits of economics of scale to the producers, as well as scope for local business to compete with imports or in the export market, in an increasingly liberalized world.

The case for homogeneity therefore appears divided. What is clear from the discussion in the preceding section is that homogeneity cannot ensure that all states retain the or existing levels of revenue. Some states seem to gain while others appear to feel the pinch of the prescribed rates. While the choice of state-specific rates world have placed the burden and benefit of such a transition on the states, the prescription of homogeneity would place the costs of sustaining it on the union government. If improved compliance is expected to bring in additional revenues in the medium term, this would be equally true for all the states. Hence the states, which expect to gain less from the transition, are encouraged to report a loss and benefit from central compensation. Once this process is initiated, there is a problem in defining the exact quantum of losses. As Tables 1 and 2 demonstrate, changes in the assumptions regarding value added subsequent to the first sale can significantly alter the amount of compensation required as well as the number of states likely to suffer a decline in revenue. Further, instituting an assessed loss based mechanism for compensation would induce the sates to collect less and seek higher levels of compensation, a classic principal-agent problem resulting in increases in the costs of compensation. Lastly, sustaining the homogeneity subsequent to the withdrawal of the compensation mechanism would be difficult since the interests of the individual states could vary widely as reflected in the tax–GSDP ratios at present.

Concluding Remarks

The attempt here has been to provide some dimensions to the extent of gain/loss to states from the introduction of VAT. The estimates indicate that the impact varies considerably across states, while some states seem to gain considerably from such a transition, in some other states the gains could onvert to losses depending on the assumptions on increments to value added . the estimates are based on the assumption of all states adopting a uniform VAT design.

One way for the states to avoid incurring losses with introduction of VAT would be through variations in the rates and or structure of tax. Variations in the tax structure, however, are being perceived as hindrances to the formation of a common national market. Clearly, the costs of imposing/assuring such a uniformity would then have to be borne by the union government. The union government's assurance for compensation would trigger off a negative response form the state where non collection is rewarded. Any methodology to distinguish between genuine losses and slack in collections would be heavily contested especially since the databases for the states are rather poor.

5

States Debt and Debt Relief

The issue of states debt has assumed greater significance especially since the mid 1990s, with the debt GDP ration rising persistently to reach a high level of reach a high level of 28.1, percent in 2002-03. in absolute terms the outstanding debt of states increased almost fivefold to Rs6,94,289 core in 2002-03, up from a level of Rs, 1,10,289 core in 1990-91. If we take the concept of extended debt, i.e. debt inclusive of probable devolvement of outstanding guarantees the increase is even more striking. In fact, the high level of debt in conjunction with the level of contingent liabilities and the rising incidence of delays/ defaults on guarantees issued by states, depicts a much more worrisome scenario. The debt build-up at the sub-national level as an indicator of fiscal distress or vulnerability has a spill-over impact on sovereign ratings by credit rating agencies.

The deterioration in fiscal performance of the states since the mid-1980s was reflected in all major fiscal indicators, viz., fiscal deficits, revenue deficit and debt-GDP ratio (Graph). The situation started worsening more rapidly since 1987-88 when the surplus on the revenue account turned negative. Gross fiscal deficit as a ratio to GDP which averaged 2.8 per cent in first half of 1980s, had risen to 3.0per cent in 1986-87 and further to 3.3 per cent in 1990-91. This was followed by a brief period of consolidation with the GFD/GDP ratio falling to 2.4 per cent by 1993-94. In the subsequent years, there was a gradual increase in the deficit and after the implementation of pay revision awards the deficit ratio recorded a sharp jump from 2.9 per cent in 1997-98 to 4.3 per cent in 1998-99 and further to 4.7per cent in 1999-2000.

The average annual growth in outstanding debt for the 1980s and the 1990s remained the same at 16.4 per cent, though the growth in first half of the 1990s, at 14.4 per cent, was much lower than the second half of the 1990s, at 18.8 per cent.

Composition of Debt

The public debt of states comprises of internal debt (including market borrowing, loans from banks and financial institutions (FIS), special securities issued to the National small saving fund (NSSF), loans from the center, and small savings and provident funds, etc. special securities issued to NSSF earlier formed part of the loans from the center, and since 1999-2000, these were classified separately and treated as part of the internal debt of the states. The finance commission excludes the short-term components of debt, viz. ways and means advances (WMA), reserve funds and deposits, in assessing the overall debt position of state governments. Although WMA and overdrafts are arrange mends to overcome temporary liquidity mismatches, they tend to get rolled over almost continuously thereby integrating with the budgetary process to become almost an additional or regular source of finance, more importantly these come at a cost-WMA being at bank rate, while OD(up to 100 per cent of WMA limit) is at bank rate +3 per cent or (more than 100per cent of WMA limit) is at bank rate +6 per cent.

Loans from the centre, which from the most important constituent of states debt are extended under two broad categories plan-loans and non-plan loans. Under plan loans, those pertaining to the centrally-sponsored scheme are the most prominent. Though state government do not have direct access to external sources, the external assistance obtained from international financial institutions/foreign governments are passed on from the center to the states as central plan assistance under the head additional entrap assistance (ACA) by recasting the original terms and conditions of the loan. Total loans from the centre amounted to Rs. 25,33,688 core in 2001-02, constituting 39.6 per cent of the total states debt. The rate of interest on central loans. Both plan and non-plan was raised continuously from 7.5per cent in 1984-85 to 20 per cent during 1995-98. It was thereafter reduced to 12.5 per cent. The change in interest rates on these loans reflect the governments efforts to align these rates with market related rates of interest. This component of the states debt is completely controlled by the center (though the consolidated fund of the state) funded through the general revenues of the state governments at rates of interest not determined by the market.

Loans from small savings collections viz., Kisan Vikas Patra, National Savings Certificate, etc. which earlier formed the major part of the non-plan loan until 1998-99 are now shown separately as special securities issued to the NSSF. This 15 the component over which the center has no control and it almost doubled from Rs 26.416 crore in 1999-00to Rs 59.022 crore in 2000-01.although the amounts lent by NSSF to the states do not appear on the centers budget the ultimate liability to repay the depositors remains that of the center. Also the cost of borrowing through this route is relatively higher as the cost of administering the schemes of small saving is added to the interest payable to depositors. Partly reflecting the lower interest rates on small savings the rate charged to states on the on-lent small saving component, which was 14 per cent per annum in 1998-99has subsequently been reduced to 9.5 per cent at present on the special securities issued to the NSSF.

Loans from banks and FIS have emerged as another important component recording a tenfold increase from Rs 2.906 crore in 1991 to Rs 32.235 crore in 2001. these include loans from Life Insurance Corporation (LIC), General Insurance Corporation (GIC), National Bank for Agriculture and Rural Development (NABARD), Rural Electrification Corporation (REC), Industrial Development Bank of India (IDBI), Housing and Urban Development Corporation (HUDCO) and other financial institutions, these are meant for specific developmental projects like housing rural roads sanitation power transport etc, and accounted for 6.5 per cent of the total liabilities as an end-march 2001. The competitive increase in plan size without matching resources resulted in an increase in plan negotiated loans contracted at high rates of interest, which varies for different states depending upon the assessment of their financial viability. Current rate of interest on negotiated loans from HUDCO and LIC are 10.5 per cent. This component of states debt is not under the market borrowing programme (MBP) but article 293 approval of the centre has to be sought by the state. Hence to that extent it is controlled by the center.

Public account liabilities are those in which the government acts as a banker accepting deposits, funds and even pays interest on them. These liabilities are unfounded implying huge risks on the budgets of states. The small savings schemes run by the states themselves and provident fund receipts form a part of the public accounts of state governments as against the other components, which are routed through the consolidated fund of state governments. The accumulation in provident fund of employees registered a sharp in the closing years of the 1990s. consequent to the pay revision with the impounding of a part of the additional emoluments of employees. This component of the states debt it is uncapped as the center has no control on it. The share of this component was 17.3 per cent at the end of march 2002. on average the interest rate on states small savings collections is currently estimated at 10.5 per cent.

Table 1: Composition of Total Debt

(Rs crore)

	1990-91	1995-96	1996-97	1997-98	1998-99	1999-00	2000-01	2001-02
1 Internal Debt								
a Market Loans	15,518 (14.2)	36,021 (17.0)	42,538 (17.5)	49,618 (17.7)	60,283 (17.6)	72,947 (17.4)	65,468 (17.2)	1,02,715 (17.5)
b Loans from Banks and FIs	2,906 (2.6)	7,225 (3.4)	8,425 (3.6)	10,847 (3.9)	13,893 (4.1)	20,132 (4.8)	32,238 (6.5)	43,916 (7.5)
c Special Securities issued to NSSF	- -	- -	- -	- -	- -	26,416 (6.3)	59,022 (11.8)	94,670 (18.1)
2 Loans and Advances from the Central Government	74,117 (67.2)	1,31,505 (62.0)	1,49,053 (61.2)	1,72,729 (61.4)	2,03,798 (59.6)	2,16,194 (51.5)	2,24,590 (45.1)	2,35,564 (40.2)
3 Small Savings, Provident Funds, etc	16,961 (15.4)	37,502 (17.7)	42,078 (17.6)	49,103 (17.5)	61,072 (17.9)	78,949 (18.8)	92,058 (18.5)	1,02,242 (17.4)
Total Debt	1,102,89	2,12,226	2,43,525	2,81,207	3,41,978	4,20,132	4,99,082	5,86,087
Contingent Liabilities		52,631	63,409	73,751	97,454	1,32,029	1,68,712	1,66,116

Note: Figures in brackets are percentages to the total - Not Available.

In recent years, market borrowings have emerged as the cheapest source of raising funds for state governments with the average rate of interest declining continuously from 14.0 per cent in 1995-96 to 6.2 per cent by march 2003. as a result its share in total liabilities of states has gone up from 14.2 per cent at end-March

1991 to 17.2 per cent at end-march 2003. however, borrowing programmed of states is finalized by the government of India in consultation with the planning commission, keeping in view the projections regarding investigable resources and other monetary parameters, made by the Reserve Bank of India (RBI).

Apart from the borrowings routed through the budget, states have also resorted to several non-transparent off-budget borrowings. State have taken resource to borrowings through public sector enterprises (PSEs) under their control, enabling them to float bonds against state government guarantees, other special purpose vehicles mainly for infrastructure financing have also come into the picture. Although contingent liabilities do not form a part of the debt of states, in the event of default by the borrowing entry, the states will be required to meet debt service obligations. At the same time non-adherence to the payment obligations committed by states, in respect of guarantees already provided by them would have adverse implication on sovereign credibility. In addition this may pose difficulties for states to raise resources from the market in future. The extant outstanding debt is therefore an incomplete picture. A more holistic measure would be the concept of extended debt, i.e., consolidated debt, taking into account the risky guarantees by assigning appropriate risk-weights in line with the probability of development on the state budget. While this idea has merits there are practical difficulties in assigning such weight ages. The technical committee on state government guarantees estimated the composite burden of public debt and guarantees, including a third of the guarantees with debt (as shown in table 2). From 2006-07 to 2015-16, repayment of power bonds is estimated to amount to Rs. 2,900 core per annum, which would further enhance the pressure of redemption on state governments. A snapshot of the states fiscal stability suitability and flexibility in terms of some simple indicative rations is presented in Table 3.

Statewise Position

The statewide debt GSDP ratio is furnished in annexes 1 to 3. which emphasizes the deteriorating debt situation of state governments. The relative position of states can be better assessed by looking at the average ration of interest payments to revenue receipts (IP-PR) along with the average debt to GSDP ratio (Average of five years 1996-97 to 2000-01) (table 4). Selectivity of IP-PR is no the grounds of conceptual simplicity as revenue receipts define the repaying capacity, while interest payments reflect the debt service of past debts. It is also a handy assessment of the level of interest payments that are to be finance through the current revenue receipts, and borrowings.

The classification of states in table 4 reflects on the current servicing capacity vis-a vis the overall debt situation. Except for Karnataka and Tamil Nadu, all the other major states displayed high levels of IP-PR on the other hand states like Punjab, utter prudish orison, Bihar hibachi prudish and karalla depict a grim scenario with both interest payments more than 15 per cent of revenue receipts and debt more than 30 per cent of GSDP. Gujarat and Maharashtra fall together in the bracket of low debt· ratio but high interest payments ratio. For special category and smaller states, the IP-PR ratio remained less than 15 per cent level (on account of higher proportion of central transfers in their revenues) but debt was above 30 per cent of the respective GSDP (except Goa and

Kerala), reflecting the weak fiscal position of the states.

Table 2: Indicators of States Fiscal Stability and Flexibility—All States

1992-93	19.0	5.7	20.9
1993-94	18.6	5.7	20.5
1994-95	18.2	4.8	19.8
1995-96	17.9	4.4	19.3
1996-97	17.8	4.6	19.3
1997-98	18.5	4.8	20.1
1998-99	19.6	5.6	21.5
1999-00	21.7	6.8	24.0
2000-01	23.7	8.0	26.3
2001-02	25.7	7.2	28.1

Table 3: Indicators of States Fiscal Stability and Flexibility—All States

1990-91	19.4	18	13	6.5	43.5
1995-96	18	0.8	16	4.4	48.9
1996-97	17.9	0.9	16.7	4.6	46.7
1997-98	18.6	0.9	17.7	4.8	46.3
1998-99	19.4	2.2	20.3	5.6	42.1
1999-00	21.7	2.4	21.7	6.8	40.8
2000-01	23.7	1.8	21.7	8.0	45.3
2001-02	25.7	1.5	24.4	7.2	43.4

What Led to Sharp Deterioration of State Finances?

There is a vast fiscal literature which has investigated the various factors leading to the deterioration of state finances. The inability to contain wasteful expenditure including subsidies, reluctance to raise additional resources and competitive reduction in taxes are attributed as the main causes of fiscal deterioration [Korean 1999]. Another study identifies the increase in the share of non-developmental expenditure, particularly rising interest payments and sluggishness of central transfers as the principal causes of deterioration in state finances [Chakraborty 1999].

Table 4: Categorisation of States Based on IP/RR and Debt/GSDP Ratios

IP-RR Ratio	Debt-GSDP Ratio: Very High (Above 50 Per Cent)	High (30-50 Per Cent)	Medium (20-30 Per Cent)	Low (Below 20 Per C...
Very High (above 25 per cent)		Punjab, Uttar Pradesh, Orissa	West Bengal, Rajasthan	
High (15-25 per cent)	Bihai, Himachal Pradesh	Kerala	Haryana, Andhra Pradesh, Madhya Pradesh, Assam	Gujarat, Maharas...
Medium (10-15 per cent)	Jammu and Kashmir, Nagaland	Tripura, Manipur	Goe	Tamil Nadu, Karna...
Low (below 10 per cent)	Mizoram, Arunachal Pradesh, Sikkim		Meghalaya	

Note: Based on averages of IP to RR and Debt to GSDP ratios for five years (1996-97 to 2000-01). The debt figures for Bihar, Madhya Pradesh and Uttar Prad... inclusive of Jharkhand, Chhattisgarh and Uttaranchal, respectively, for 1999-2000 and 2000-01.

Rakish Mohan (2002) points out that increasing debt service payments and inadequate returns from government spending are the major factors beheld the deteriorating fiscal conditions of states. Since there is no link between the capacity to borrows and the return on services provided by government, there does not exist much incentive for the governments to levy appropriate user changes. In fact the lack of connection between fiscal health and ability to borrow has encouraged fiscally irresponsible behaviour on the part of the states.

Detailed analysis of fiscal trends by Gavin Rao (2002) and Shankerchary (2002) illustrate the implementation of the fifth pay commission wards as a major cause of sharp deterioration in state finances. It has been further argued that the inadequate increase in central transfers coupled with slow growth in states own (non-tax and tax) revenue had its impact on states fiscal situation. While, slow growth in transfers reflects the precariousness of the center own finances, inability to affect proper cost recoveries from public services and generate adequate returns from public investments. The deceleration in tax revenue was mainly on account of the inability of states to tax services and agricultural income as also competitive reeducation in taxes through exemption schemes.

Anand et al (2001) identify both demand and supply side factors for the worsening fiscal situation. All populist factors appear on the demand side while softening of the budget constraint implicit in constitutional restrictions on borrowings would appear on the supply side. Four factors are identified to cause softening of the hard budget constraint viz, increased small savings borrowing through state level public sector units (PSUS), accumulation of large arrears by state electricity boards to central agencies and rolling over of short term accommodation provided by the RBI in the form of WMA.

The RBI study of state Budgets 2002-03 while drawing attention to the growing fiscal and revenue deficit and high debt levels of states has pointed towards reason such as inadequate increase in tax receipts negative or negligible returns from public investments due to PSU losses, large subsidy payments increase in expenditure on salaries due to pay revisions higher-pension outgo etc.

From the foregoing survey of literature prominent factors resulting in the deterioration of state finance could be identified. These include inadequate increase in resources growing proportion of non-developmental expenditure on wages. Salaries and pensions interest payments, lower user charges and slowdown in central transfers.

Since there are large disparities in terms of the level of income and tax and expenditure policies pursued by respective state governments, the impact of various factors identified above would vary across states. Thus there is need to track the changes both over the period and across the states. Taking into account these considerations, in a recent empirical analysis, panel data was taken to study factors affecting state finances. The exercise attempted to quantify the relative strength of each of the of the above four factors which appeared to have worsened state finances during the past two decades. Results of the panel for 15 major states are set out as below 2.

Period 1980-81 to 1989-90;

GFD/GDP= 0.61 IP GDP+3 08.TFR –1.18 COSTR +0.88 WAGE/GDP

(0.56) (4.03) (2.95) (2.15)

period 1990-91 to 1999-00

GFD/GDP =0.35 IP /GDP TFR-0.35 COSTR+0.25 WAGE /GDP

(2.18) (5.12) (3.75) (1.81)

Results indicate that all the factors (except interest payments), viz. user changes, wages and salaries and central transfers significantly influenced the fiscal outcome in both the 1980s and 1990s. Interest payments, on the other hand came into prominence only in the 1990s. During the period up to the mid-1980s, interest rates on government borrowings were highly subsidized, since then interest on government bonds were progressively aligned to market interest rates. The average interest rate on rate government bonds rose from 6.75 to 9.75 per cent during the early 1980s, to 11.00 to 11.50 per cent in late 1980s, and further to 11.00 to 14.00 per cent during the 1990s, similarly reliance on market loans for financing fiscal deficit rose from 11 per cent in the 1980s to 16 per cent in the 1990s, significant changes in the structure and cost of state government debt led to sharp increases in interest payments during the 1990s, despite the softening interest rates in the latter half of the 1990s. This is because states had to pay the cost on past borrowings or the inherited component of debt contracted at a higher cost.

Table 5: Impact of Spread and Primary Deficit On Debt-GDP Ratio

Primary Deficit (PD) And Quantum Spread (QS)	*Fiscal Imbalance (QS+PD)*	*Debt–GDP Ratio*
PD =QS	To	Constant
PD >QS	>To	Rising
PD <QS	<To	Falling

Debt Dynamics and Role of Interest Payments

Debt is essentially the aggregate of borrowing made by the government to finance its fiscal deficit over the years. Therefore, higher the fiscal deficit larger would be additions to the debt stock. It is quite apparent from the empirical evidence that interest payments have been the key factor causing sharp increases in states gross fiscal deficit and rapid growth in outstanding debt, of state governments. Thus efforts to contain growth in debt accumulation or to bring state government debt on a sustainable path would require a deistic reduction in the interest burden. This brings us to the following questions what is the criterion for debt sustainability?

What are the dimension of the interest burden at present? How much reduction in interest burden is required and what are the options available to reduce it so as to make debt sustainable? And more importantly is the policy of debt restructuring to reduce burden alone sufficient to achieve the sustainable debt path? The present section attempts to answer these question.

In simple terms sustainability is defined as the ability to maintain a constant debt–GDP radio over a period of time. Sustainability is challenged when the debt to –GDP radio reaches an excessive value. Blanchard et al define sustainable fiscal policy as the one that allows, in the short term, debt to GDP ratio to return to its original level after some excessive variation. Traditionally debt sustainability is measured in terms of Do mars equation. Which states that public debt is sustainable as long as the rate of growth of income exceeds the interest Tate or cost of public borrowings, subject to the condition that the primary balance is either positive or zero. This condition can be stated as below:

$$\Delta d = d (r - g) - z$$

where

z = Primary balance as a share of GDP, d =debt-GDP ratio,

g = income growth rate, and r = interest rate.

It may be noted that the above equation does not imply that this primary deficits has to be zero at all times if debt –GDP ratio has to remain constant. A stable debt –GDP ratio could be achieved with the primary deficit. Provided it is lower than the spread between growth in GDP and the interest rate. To understand this point more clearly, the following three terms could be defined;

Rate spread = GDP growth rate-interest Rate

Quantum spread =Debt (1(* Rate Spread

Fiscal Imbalance =Quantum spread =primary Deficit

It could be derived from Do mars condition of debt sustainability that if quantum spread together with primary deficit is zero debt GDP ratio would remain constant. Thus the impact of spread and primary deficit on the debt –GDP ratio could be determined as per table 5.

If the spread between interest and income growth rates narrows down or if the primary balance becomes negative, fiscal imbalance (QS+PD) would be positive and addition to debt would take place at a rate faster than the growth rate of income. This would eventually reflect in rising debt-GDP ratio and debt would become unsustainable.

The essential condition which emerges from above is that fiscal imbalance must be zero, or less if the debt –GDP ratio has to stabilize or statc falling.

Current Trends

Table 6 sets out relative movements in the GDP growth rate, interest rate and gross primary deficit. The average interest rate has been proxies by the ratio of interest payments in period t to the outstanding public debt in period t-1.

It can be seen from table 6 that while the sufficient condition that primary balance should be zero or positive was never fulfilled even the necessary condition that rate of interest should be lower than growth rate of income has been violated since 1997-98. as a result the growth rate of debt exceeds the rate of growth of GDP and there has been a persistent rise in the debt GDP ratio since 1997-98. It may be mentioned that the failure of interest payments to fall commensurately with the fall in GDP growth rates and rise in primary deficit in the recent years, were the primary reasons for the sharp rise in the recent years were the primary reasons for the sharp rise in the debt GDP ratio. Notably in the average interest rate has not only have come down sharply the average interest rate has not only been higher than the current market interest rate, it has also exceeded the GDP growth rate. This essentially reflect the overhang of high cost borrowings of the past, particularly the first half of the 1990s.

Dimensions of Fiscal Imbalance

To ascertain the dimensions of fiscal imbalance at present and to determine the likely trends in the medium term, if the present policy stance continues we have generated a base line scenario under following assumptions;

Real GDP growth rate = 7 per cent

Inflation = 4 per cent

Average Interest Rate = 9.5 per cent

On fresh borrowings

Primary Deficit = 1.7 per cent of GDP

Although the tenth plan has targeted a real GDP growth rate of 8 per cent, relatively conservative view has been taken by assuming a growth rate of 7 per cent per annum throughout our projection period. Similarly it has been assumed that the average interest rate on fresh borrowings by the states would continue at the current level of 9.5 per cent (borrowings under the market borrowing programmed have been envisaged at 6 per cent and the remaining non-market borrowings including negotiated loans loans and advances by the central government and small savings are assumed at 10.5 per cent). Lastly it is assumed that the primary deficit as a proportion of GDP, wound stay at 1.7 per cent the level of the revised estimates for 2002-03. These assumptions for the baseline scenario envisage the continuation of the prevailing policy stance and any deterioration from this indicative scenario would correspondingly call for larger restructuring efforts.

Table 6: Trends in Indicators of Debt Sustainability of States

1990-91	9.2	17.0	1.8	19.4
1991-92	9.9	14.8	1.2	19.3
1992-93	10.5	14.6	1.0	19.0
1993-94	11.1	14.8	0.5	18.6
1994-95	12.1	17.9	0.8	18.2
1995-96	11.9	17.3	0.8	17.9
1996-97	12.1	15.2	0.9	17.8
1997-98	12.4	11.3	0.9	18.5
1998-99	12.8	14.3	2.2	19.6
1999-00	13.2	11.3	2.4	21.7
2000-01	12.3	8.6	1.8	23.7
2001-02	12.5	9.1	1.5	25.7
2002-03RE	12.6	7.7	1.7	28.1

Notes: Indicates a deficit.

Base–Line Scenario

This scenario shows that if the present policy stance continues, the level of fiscal imbalance would keep on rising and the debt GDP ratio would not converge even after 15 years.

In the best year (2002-03), the average interest rate on fresh state government borrowings a 9.5 per cent is lower than the average interest cost of 12.2 per cent of outstanding debt. If the current rate of fresh borrowings continues, the overall average rate on the debt stock would come down to 10.1 per cent by 2007-08 and 9.6 per cent by the end of 2017-18. This is because, in each year a part of the outstanding debt would get replaced by fresh debt and the overall interest rate on outstanding stock of debt would tend to align itself to the rate on fresh borrowings. Thus the GDP growth rate would have a positive spread of 0.9 per cent over the overall average interest rate in the year 2007-08. and would rise further to 1.4 per cent in 2017-18. Accordingly, the quantum spreads would amount to Rs.12.019 crore and s 75.434 crore in the respective years. However these amounts would be insufficient to neutralize the primary deficit in corresponding years, which under the assumption of 1.7 per cent of GDP would grow at a faster pace. Thus the size of the fiscal imbalance would continue to rise and debt–GDP ratio would not converge even after 15 yeas.

Thus attaining sustainability would necessitate either of the following:

(i) spread between interest rate and GDP growth rate increased further to accommodate the prevailing primary deficit, for a given income level, this would essentially require debt-structuring measures such as debt-swaps and lowering of interest cost on fresh borrowings.

(ii) Alternatively, the level of the primary deficit itself has to be reduced to the level equivalent to the spread between the interest rate and GDP growth rate. This indicates the need for fiscal restructurings. With a view to assess and prescribe probable policy initiatives to bring states debt on the sustainable path three sets of alternative policy scenarios have been generated by superimposing the alternative assumptions over the baseline scenario. The first two policy scenarios envisage debt-restructuring measures so as to increase the spread between interest rate and GDP growth rate. The last scenario envisages a reduction in the primary deficit in addition to the debt–restructuring measure assumed in the preceding scenarios. Three scenarios are as below:

(iii) Entire central government Debt is swapped with fresh market borrowings.

(iv) (1) plus reduction in interest rate on non-market borrowings.

(v) (2) plus progressive reduction in primary deficit.

Policy Scenario 1: Debt Restructuring–Debt Swap

Debt restructuring involves a combination of debt conversion and debt reduction strategies by employing instruments like debt-swap debt buy–back and debt relief. In case of debt–swap there is a substitution of high cost past debt with fresh debt at current market rates of interest. Though there is no reduction in the size of the debt- considerable reduction in the interest payments would reduce the size of future fresh borrowings.

Since there is no put or call option attached to the liabilities of state governments restructuring of debt could be possible only through the debt swap scheme (what is often termed as within the family approach). The union government has announced a debt–swap scheme that would enable states to prepay their high cost debt. Under the mutually agreed scheme between the central and state governments, all state loans from the center bearing coupons in excess of 13 per cent would be swapped with market borrowings and small savings proceeds at prevailing interest rates over a period of three years ending in 2004-05.

The first scenario has been generated assuming that states are allowed to replace the entire liability owed to the center through fresh low cost market borrowings at the assumed rate of 6.0 per cent. As result, overall interest rate on the debt stock comes down to 10.0 per cent in 2007–08 and further to 9.5 per cent by 2017-18. accordingly rate and quantum spread improves over the baseline scenario however they continue to e inadequate to accommodate the primary deficit in the corresponding period. As a result the size of the fiscal imbalance keeps on rising and debt GDP ratio fails to converge even after a 15-years period. Thus debt swap alone would not be a sufficient solution for bringing state debt onto a sustainable path.

Policy Scenario 2: Debt Restructuring–Debt Swap Plus Reduction in Interest Rates

Non-market borrowings of the states as set out above mainly include plan and non-plan loans extended by the central government, negotiated loans raised from banks/FIS and small savings. Average interest rates on each of these components exceeds 10 per cent-far above the interest rate on market loans. So another probable policy initiative could to be to align the interest rates on this component of state borrowings to the market rate under this scenario. In addition to the debt swap (policy scenario 1) interest rates on non-market borrowings are also reduced so that the average interest rate on these borrowings is only 100 basis points above the assumed market interest rate of 6.0 per cent.

Under the above assumptions the average interest rate on the debt stock falls sharply to 8.7 per cent in 2007-08 and further to 7.3 per cent by 2017-18. with the result there is a conceding policy scenario 1. but they still fall short of the primary deficits in the respective years. The improvement in spreads shows up in the falling fiscal imbalance and translates into slower growth in the debt-GDP ratio but the latter fails to converge even after a 15-year period.

Extended scenario 2: it could be pointed out tat in view of the softer interest rate regime, interest rate could fall below the assumed rate of 6 percent. Under such a scenario, the spread could be higher and the debt-GDP ratio may converge. To examine this further simulations with a lower interest rate falls to 3 per cent even then the debt–GDP ratio would converge only after 10 years. Further if it is desired that debt GDP ratio must converge by 2007-08, coinciding with the term of the 12 the finance commission, the market rate needs to be reduced to the unrealistically low level of 0.25 percent. These results only further strengthen the earlier stated proposition that debt restructuring is no solution for bringing states debt onto a sustainable path. Thus the policy envisaging reduction in the interest burden by way of both debt-swaps and cut in interest rates on fresh borrowings in the future would not bring about the desirable result.

Policy Scenario 3: Debt and Fiscal Restructuring

Under this scenario, along with debt restructuring measures of scenario2, policy initiatives towards fiscal restructuring have also been envisaged. This scenario acumens that the primary deficit of the states from the current level of 1.66 per cent of GDP is progressively reduced by 0.1 percentage points each year.

Accordingly, the primary deficit falls to 0.9 per cent of GDP by 2010-11. This amounts to about Rs.55.000 crore which is also equal to the quantum spread in that year. Thus the fiscal imbalance gets reduced to zero and the debt–GDP ratio converges at 31.8 per cent. Faster convergence gene could be achieved with higher fiscal correction. A highest reduction of 0.2 percentage points in the primary deficit each year would bring the states debt on a sustainable path within a span of 5 years, i.e., by 2007-08.

The following conclusions could be drawn from the above analysis.

(1) The impact of the debt-swap is only marginal and insufficient for attaining convergence of the debt-GDP ratio.

(2) Aligning the interest rate reduces the overall interest cost and does slow down growth in the debt-GDP ratio considerably but sustainability cannot still be achieved if the market interest rate continues to be assumed at the level of 6 per cent.

(3) If the market interest rate falls to the 3.0 per cent level and interest on the non- market component of borrowings is kept 100 basis points above that the debt GDP ratio would converge after 10 years even without fiscal restructuring. If convergence has to be brought within 5 years the market rate must fall to the unrealistically low level of 0.25 per cent.

(4) Along with debt restructuring if the primary deficit as a percentage of GDP is also reduced by .1 percentage points per annum, the debt-GDP ratio would converge by 2010-11 and in case the primary deficit is reduced by 0.2 percentage points, the debt–GDP ratio would converge by 2007-08.

It could be inferred from the above scenario analysis

that lowering of the primary deficit beside reduction in interest cost should be the integral part of any policy for envisaging debt sustainability at the state level. Reeducation in the primary deficit would call for fiscal restructuring by way of enhancing the tax revenue, user changes on investment and by pruning subsidies, the size of the government etc. Similarly policy initiatives would also be required to lower the prevailing market Ris perception of state government bonds, which inter alia affects the cost of borrowings by the states. While the reduction in the primary deficit would itself have a salutary impact, other policy initiatives such as the creation of a sinking fund, transparency, adoption of stricter prudential norms, etc, would also be required to reduce the risk perception and thereby cost of borrowings.

Trends in key macroeconomic variables under different scenarios are presented in Annexure 4 to 7, and are summarized in Table 7:

Thus, the reduction in states' debt would require a two–pronged approach focusing on both quantum as well as cost of fresh borrowings. From the issuers' end, i.e. the state governments. This would entail efforts to reduce the primary fiscal gap and putting mechanisms in place to lower subscribers risk perception on state paper, and thereby the cost of borrowings.

Most of the measures on reduction in primary fiscal gap such as reduction on wasteful expedition, enhanced returns from state PSUs. Increased revenues by appropriate user charges, expansion of tax base, pension reforms, disinvestments, etc., are well researched and documented and need not be enumerated to avoid repetition. As regards cost of borrowings, one needs to distinguish between market ad non-market borrowings.

Non-market borrowings which mainly include funds received from the central government. NSSF and states own small savings are generally extended at administered interest rates. In recent years, there is a tendency to align these rates to the hand, reflects the risk perception of state paper apart from overall market conditions. In the following section, the issues related to administered interest rates on non market borrowings and risk perception on state paper have been outlined.

Non-Market Borrowings

Central transfers: with regard to the reduction in the interest burden, an important area which needs to be addressed is the interest rate on funds for centrally sponsored schemes (CSS) and those for externally aided projects (EAP). Significantly these two together account for a sizeable proportion of the total fresh loans and advances from the central government. It could be noted that the interest cost on central loans at present exceeds 10 percent. Aligning the interest rate on these funds with the actual cost (of central government) could make a major dent in the interest burden of the states.

Annexure 1: Debt/GSDP Ratio of States

States	*1995-96*	*1996-97*	*1997-98*	*1998-99*	*1999-00*	*2000-01*
Andhra Pradesh	19.0	19.1	20.8	20.8	23.5	25.9
Arunachal Pradesh	53.5	58.0	58.2	56.7	56.7	54.6
Assam	28.1	27.8	27.2	26.7	29.3	33.2
Bihar	67.7	55.9	59.9	59.7	66.9	73.1
Goa	35.2	32.3	28.6	27.7	28.5	32.7
Gujarat	15.5	14.9	16.6	17.8	21.6	26.6
Haryana	19.4	18.3	19.7	53.4	23.9	24.5
Himachal Pradesh	45.4	44.2	44.9	21.8	54.0	60.8
Jammu & Kashmir	56.5	55.6	56.9	50.4	55.5	61.5
Karnataka	17.6	17.4	18.1	17.6	19.5	21.0
Kerala	26.1	25.7	26.0	27.9	32.3	34.6
Madhya Pradesh	25.7	25.4	26.7	28.0	30.4	36.2

Maharashtra	11.6	12.3	13.3	14.6	15.9	17.3
Manipur	34.9	31.3	39.0	44.0	44.6	51.2
Meghalaya	21.7	22.0	22.4	24.2	26.5	28.9
Mizoram	44.5	47.2	52.9	58.6	62.7	62.2
Nagaland	51.8	52.5	51.1	57.8	64.5	
Orissa	35.3	42.1	39.2	44.2	50.5	60.5
Punjab	35.3	34.5	35.3	37.4	37.9	40.7
Rajasthan	25.8	25.4	25.6	28.9	33.3	40.1
Skim	57.5	56.6	54.8	64.5	80.6	80.2
Tamil Nadu	16.0	15.8	15.7	16.4	18.7	20.9
Tripura	37.0	35.4	34.1	36.4	39.2	44.8
Uttar Pradesh	28.2	26.9	29.2	31.5	35.2	36.7
West Bengal	20.8	22.1	22.5	24.8	28.9	33.7
Total	17.9	17.8	18.5	19.6	21.7	23.7

Source: Report on currency and finance, volume II and state Finances various issues. Reserve bank of India.

Indicator year end	*Initi period*	*Basic line scenario*		*Policy scenario 1*		*Policy scenario 2*		*Policy scenario 3*	
	2003	*2008*	*2018*	*2008*	*2018*	*2008*	*2018*	*2008*	*2018*
Real GDP	7.0	7.0	7.0	7.0	7.0	7.0	7.0	7.0	7.0
Inlation	4.0	4.0	4.0	4.0	4.0	4.0	4.0	4.0	4.0
Pr Def	1.7	1.7	1.7	1.7	1.7	1.7	1.7	1.2	0.9
Avg Int	12.2	10.1	9.6	10.0	9.5	8.7	7.3	8.8	8.0
D-Y Ratio	25.9	33.8	45.9	33.7	45.3	32.7	38.7	31.2	31.7
Rate Spread	-1.2	0.9	1.4	1.0	1.5	2.3	3.7	2.2	3.6
Quantum spread	-7391	12042	75619	13319	78879	30669	171414	29046	127762

Likewise, states themselves could set up other debt amortization funds towards redemptions, liabilities/ loans other than market borrowings, i.e., loans from banks and FIs, public account liabilities and liabilities on account of nssf. The fund should not used for any their purpose except for redemption of such loans used for any other purpose except for redemption of such loans. Initially, to set up the fund, states may keep aside a modest 1 to 3 percent of their fresh accretions of all such loans, particularly accruing on NSSF/public accounts. The find should be clearly kept to of the purview of the states' consolidated fund and public account.

Ceiling on guarantees and guarantee redemption fund: Given the deterioration in state finances over the years, which has led to erosion in public investment, state governments have taken recourse to loan guarantees promote investments. Although the contingent liabilities do not form a part of the debt burden of states, in the event of default by the borrowing entity, states are required to meet the debt service obligations. At the same time, non-adherence to payment obligations committee by states in respect of guarantees already provided my them would have adverse implications on sovereign creditability. In addition, this my pose difficulties for states to raise resources from the market in future. There is a provision of placing limits on guarantees under Article 293 and the Reserve Bank of India has taken several initiatives to contain the growth in guarantees extended by state governments, like encouraging states to impose ceilings on guarantees, introduction of guarantee fees and the constitution of a contingency fund or GRF (guarantee redemption fund). Goa, Gujarat, Karnataka, Rajasthan, Assam, Sikkim, and West Bengal have introduced ceiling on guarantees. The issue of imposing ceiling on guarantees is under active consideration in Tamil Nadu and Kerala, Likewise, Andhra Pradesh, Orissa, Haryana and Gujarat set up GRFs and earmarked guarantee fees towards the fund.

Annexure 2: Interest Payments Revenue Reciepts Ratios State-wise

States	*1995-96*	*1996-97*	*1997-98*	*1998-99*	*1999-00*	*2000-01*
Andhra Pradesh	15.5	16.4	15.6	18.5	18.	19.5
Arunachal Pradesh	5.6	6.6	7.2	7.7	7.8	12.6
Assam	14.4	14.5	14.8	11.6	19.7	15.3
Bihar	22.6	17.6	17.7	20.2	22.7	20.9
Goa	11.0	12.4	10.7	12.5	14.5	14.3
Gujarat	15.5	16.7	16.9	17.8	20.2	19.9

Haryana	11.1	11.8	13.9	18.2	23.5	22.7
Himachal Pradesh	16.3	15.7	17.1	21.5	16.1	26.2
Jammu & Kashmir	13.5	13.3	13.8	14.7	15.3	15.6
Karnataka	12.3	12.6	13.1	14.4	15.6	16.1
Kerala	17.0	18.0	18.1	20.1	246	25.9
Madhya Pradesh	13.4	13.7	14.7	16.2	16.2	17.6
Maharashtra	12.4	12.7	14.3	16.9	19.3	17.7
Manipur	8.3	8.1	9.1	10.2	12.3	17.0
Meghalaya	7.4	7.6	8.7	8.3	10.1	10.0
Mizoram	5.6	7.1	9.1	10.0	9.8	12.2
Nagaland	10.2	11.2	11.4	13.2	14.3	13.7
Orissa	23.9	25.2	27.9	32.6	21.0	33.1
Punjab	28.7	29.4	29.1	40.3	35.3	25.0
Rajasthan	16.2	20.5	22.6	26.1	28.9	26.9
Sikkim	3.1	2.9	3.1	3.6	4.5	9.1
Tamil Nadu	12.2	12.3	13.0	14.9	16.6	17.1
Tripura	9.5	10.7	11.1	11.1	12.9	13.8
Uttar Pradesh	21.9	25.3	26.7	31.7	30.5	30.1
West Bengal	21.9	23.6	26.7	31.4	40.8	36.1
Total	16.0	16.7	17.7	20.3	21.8	21.7

Source: State Finance various issues, Reserve Bank of India.

Transparency: Transparency at sub-national level, with regard to budgeting, accounting and auditing practices, would enable investors to make informed judgements about the repaying capacity of the government. Uniform, consistent reporting formats would enable provision of consolidated data on important fiscal indicators. State governments should achieve a minimum set of standards of transparency within a stipulated time frame, and should be encouraged to increase the extent of reporting on contingent liabilities and at least, major tax expenditures and quasi fiscal activities (specially losses of state electricity boards, (SEBs).

Fiscal responsibility and political consensus: The advantage of a rule based fiscal policy in instilling investor confidence over a discretionary one, is well recognized. Fiscal consolidation is no longer dependent upon political consensus, if there are binding fiscal rules/

legislation in force. States can consider implementing a mix of legislations relating to balanced budgets, caps on deficit. Debt restrictions on borrowings, etc. While the states of Karnataka, Punjab and Tamil Nadu have already enacted the fiscal responsibility legislation, Kerala has passed a fiscal accountability bill and Maharashtra has introduced the bill in its legislature.

Annexure 3: Statewise Primary Deficit

States	*1995-96*	*1996-97*	*1997-98*	*1998-99*	*1999-00*	*2000-01*
Andhra Pradesh	888	973	275	3062	1875	3513
Arunachal Pradesh	-3	17	61	-16	-20	89
Assam	165	-486	-497	-182	650	675
Bihar	-97	-526	-555	507	3246	2510
Goa	7	4	7	125	163	201
Gujarat	418	748	1290	3357	3984	4856
Haryana	430	384	307	1243	775	773
Himachal Pradesh	236	259	830	1163	-408	1047
Jamu kashmir	-344	-323	-149	390	494	1322
Karnataka	409	736	216	1495	2264	1832
Kerala	379	439	1128	1566	2584	1620
Madhya Pradesh	475	550	161	2292	1773	301
Maharashtra	2095	550	3539	3789	6823	3751
Manipur	47	2506	109	15	524	57
Meghalaya	2	102	66	78	113	136
Mizoram	36	-33	58	59	85	274
Nagaland	152	78	91	107	86	165
Orissa	467	86	511	1431	2508	1038
Punjab	-125	523	629	1463	558	1560
Rajasthan	1341	-170	655	2908	2536	974
Sikkim	11	953	26	94	25	-28
Tamil Nadu	-37	23	358	2655	2671	1952
Tripura	-55	11969	76	-22	105	219
Uttar Pradesh	1056	1895	2887	6116	4546	2724
West Bengal	1080	1457	1598	4159	7497	5671
NCR Delhi	462	500	412	527	851	893
Total	9493	11675	14087	38380	46309	37830

Infrastructure financing : Whatever be the restrictions placed on the issuance of fresh debt, the inflows for infrastructure financing must not be curtailed; three-fourths of the combined development expenditure of the government is borne by the states, while the share of states in combined revenues is merely one-third. It would be useful if the fresh borrowings could be earmarked for infrastructure project and repayments could be escrowed from the revenues stream generated by such projects. The explicit tying up of repayments with the revenue stream would act as credit enhancement and would reduce the cost of funds for the states. States could also explore the possibilities of getting financing through public--private partnerships.

Annexure 4: Baseline Projections

Year	Debt	Old Debt	Debt Relief	PD/ GDP	Primary Deficit	Interest Payments	Fresh Debt	AVG INT (Tot Liab)	Avg Int (Fresh Borr)	Mkt Int	GDP Growth	Rate Spread	Quantum Spread	Fiscal Imbalance	Debt-GDP Ratio
2003-04	860788	664741	30000	1.66	51733	83855	160047	11.6	9.5	6.0	11.0	-0.6	-4083	55817	27.6
2004-05	1012651	794635	30000	1.66	57424	94439	180016	11.0	9.5	6.0	11.0	0.0	248	57175	29.3
2005-06	1183234	943115	27000	1.66	63741	106843	213115	10.6	9.5	6.0	11.0	0.4	4545	59182	30.8
2006-07	1375359	1132538		1.66	70752	121372	241820	10.3	9.5	6.0	11.0	0.7	6783	61969	[illegible]
2007-08	1590141	1317593		1.66	78535	139249	275540	10.1	9.5	6.0	11.0	0.9	13042	66483	33.7
2007-09	1839691	1526229		1.66	87174	159576	313662	10.0	9.5	6.0	11.0	1.0	16009	71094	35.0
2007-10	2119320	1762616		1.66	96763	182672	356710	9.9	9.5	6.0	11.0	1.1	19718	77547	36.4
2007-11	2435620	2030314		1.66	107407	208867	405306	9.9	9.5	6.0	11.0	1.1	24239	83168	37.5
2007-12	2793459	2333324		1.66	119221	238618	460135	9.8	9.5	6.0	11.0	1.2	29590	89321	38.9
2007-13	3198104	2676134		1.66	132336	272309	521970	9.7	9.5	6.0	11.0	1.3	34572	97364	40.1
2007-14	3655456	3063784		1.66	146893	310459	591672	9.7	9.5	6.0	11.0	1.3	41332	105560	41.3
2007-15	4172135	3501927		1.66	163051	353629	670209	9.7	9.5	6.0	11.0	1.3	48472	114579	42.5
2007-16	4755568	3996906		1.66	180987	402448	758682	9.8	9.5	6.0	11.0	1.4	56485	124498	43.6
2007-17	5414079	4555834		1.66	200895	457615	858245	9.8	9.5	6.0	11.0	1.4	65456	135399	44.7
2007-18	6157003	5186088		1.66	222994	519930	970315	9.8	9.5	6.0	11.0	1.4	75819	147375	45.8

Annexure 5: Policy Scenario 1: Debt Restructuring – Debt Swap

Year	Debt	Old Debt	Debt Relief	PD/ GDP	Primary Deficit	Interest Payments	Fresh Debt	AVG INT (Tot Liab)	Avg Int (Fresh Borr)	Mkt Int	GDP Growth	Rate Spread	Quantum Spread	Fiscal Imbalance	Debt-GDP Ratio
2003-04	860788	664741	30000	1.66	51733	83855	160047	11.58	9.50	6.00	11.0	-0.50	-4083	55817	27.6
2004-05	1012651	794635	30000	1.66	57424	94439	180016	10.97	9.50	6.00	11.0	0.03	248	57176	29.3
2005-06	1183234	943115	27000	1.66	63741	106843	213115	10.55	9.50	6.00	11.0	0.45	4549	59192	30.4
2006-07	1375359	1103538	30000	1.66	70752	121372	241530	10.26	9.50	6.00	11.0	0.74	6753	61960	[illegible]
2007-08	1591864	1290593	30000	1.66	78535	137970	274270	10.03	9.50	6.00	11.0	0.97	13213	65214	[illegible]
2007-09	1836359	1492005	30000	1.66	87174	157022	311264	9.86	9.50	6.00	11.0	1.14	18020	69056	35.0
2007-10	2111640	1728945	30000	1.66	96763	178818	352995	9.74	9.50	6.00	11.0	1.26	23149	73611	36.4
2007-11	2422738	1992651	30000	1.66	107407	203692	399787	9.65	9.50	6.00	11.0	1.35	28528	78810	37.4
2007-12	2773982	2320983		1.66	119221	232023	452909	9.58	9.50	6.00	11.0	1.42	34479	84253	38.6
2007-13	3171631	2657475		1.66	132336	265313	514155	9.56	9.50	6.00	11.0	1.44	39836	92510	39.8
2007-14	3621538	3038422		1.66	146893	303014	583118	9.55	9.50	6.00	11.0	1.45	46365	101028	40.9
2007-15	4130272	3469435		1.66	163051	345664	662636	9.56	9.50	6.00	11.0	1.45	52586	110367	[illegible]
2007-16	4705204	3956801		1.66	180987	393915	748403	9.54	9.50	6.00	11.0	1.46	60365	120601	43.2
2007-17	5354596	4507535		1.66	200895	448497	847031	9.53	9.50	6.00	11.0	1.47	69075	131820	44.3
2007-18	6087716	5129763		1.66	222994	510125	958013	9.53	9.50	6.00	11.0	1.47	78879	144114	45.3

Annexure 6. Policy Scenario 2 – Debt Restructuring, Debt Swap plus Reduction in Interest Rates on Non-Market Borrowings

Year	Debt	Old Debt	Debt Relief	PD/GDP	Primary Deficit	Interest Payments	Fresh Debt	AVG INT (Tot Liab)	Avg Int (Fresh Borr)	Mkt Int	GDP Growth	Rate Spread	Quantum Spread	Fiscal Imbalance	Debt/GDP Ratio
2003-04	860788	664741	30000	1.66	51733	83555	165047	11.6	7.0	6.0	11.0	-0.5	-4080	55817	[illegible]
2004-05	1008500	794035	30000	1.66	57424	90288	183965	10.5	7.0	6.0	11.0	0.5	4399	53025	[illegible]
2005-06	1170260	839143	27000	1.66	63741	98019	204117	9.7	7.0	6.0	11.0	1.3	12316	50825	[illegible]
2006-07	1348198	1091109	30000	1.66	70752	107187	227090	9.2	7.5	6.0	11.0	1.5	21542	[illegible]	[illegible]
2007-08	1544367	1261574	30000	1.66	78535	117633	252792	8.7	7.0	6.0	11.0	2.3	30669	[illegible]	[illegible]
2007-09	1761111	1449503	30000	1.66	87174	129571	281909	8.4	7.0	6.0	11.0	2.6	40310	46864	[illegible]
2007-10	2000990	1657144	30000	1.66	96763	143124	313854	8.1	7.0	6.0	11.0	2.9	50598	46165	[illegible]
2007-11	2256849	1888958	30000	1.66	107407	158445	349833	7.9	7.0	6.0	11.0	3.1	61655	45742	[illegible]
2007-12	2561778	2171642		1.66	119221	175707	390136	7.8	7.0	6.0	11.0	3.2	73646	45575	[illegible]
2007-13	2888751	2454183		1.66	132336	195637	435567	7.6	7.0	6.0	11.0	3.4	85159	46177	[illegible]
2007-14	3254553	2768381		1.66	146893	217910	486172	7.5	7.0	6.0	11.0	3.5	99953	[illegible]	[illegible]
2007-15	3660394	3117862		1.66	163051	242790	542532	7.5	7.0	6.0	11.0	3.5	115211	[illegible]	[illegible]
2007-16	4111950	3506657		1.66	180987	270570	605293	7.4	7.0	6.0	11.0	3.6	132074	49912	[illegible]
2007-17	4614422	3939248		1.66	200895	301576	675173	7.3	7.0	6.0	11.0	3.7	150738	50157	[illegible]
2007-18	5173587	4420610		1.66	222994	336172	752972	7.3	7.0	6.0	11.0	3.7	171414	51549	[illegible]

Annexure 7: Policy Scenario 3 – Debt and Fiscal Restructuring

Year	Debt	Old Debt	Debt Relief	PD/GDP	Primary Deficit	Interest Payments	Fresh Debt	AVG INT (Tot Liab)	Avg Int (Fresh Borr)	Mkt Int	GDP Growth	Rate Spread	Quantum Spread	Fiscal Imbalance	Debt/GDP Ratio
2003-04	857671	664741	30000	1.56	46617	83855	162930	11.5	7.0	6.0	11.0	-0.6	-4083	52700	[illegible]
2004-05	998246	791648	30000	1.46	50505	90070	176597	10.5	7.0	6.0	11.0	0.5	4274	46271	[illegible]
2005-06	1147766	829320	27000	1.36	52221	97298	191446	9.7	7.0	6.0	11.0	1.3	12509	39712	[illegible]
2006-07	1307970	1085559	30000	1.26	53703	105601	207511	9.2	7.0	6.0	11.0	1.8	20653	33060	[illegible]
2007-08	1476681	1222173	30000	1.18	54680	114731	224508	8.8	7.0	6.0	11.0	2.2	29046	25837	[illegible]
2007-09	1657141	1384660	30000	1.06	55695	124795	242491	8.5	7.0	6.0	11.0	2.5	37640	18025	[illegible]
2007-10	1848892	1557541	30000	0.96	55958	135792	261351	8.2	7.0	6.0	11.0	2.3	46494	9165	[illegible]
2007-11	2052281	1741238	30000	0.88	55644	147725	281023	8.0	7.0	6.0	11.0	3.0	55953	9	[illegible]
2007-12	2287439	1966086		0.78	54583	160595	301373	7.8	7.0	6.0	11.0	3.2	65154	-10570	[illegible]
2007-13	2495001	2172207		0.68	52615	174046	322794	7.7	7.0	6.0	11.0	3.3	74472	-21657	[illegible]
2007-14	2734749	2390211		0.58	49554	190194	344539	7.6	7.0	6.0	11.0	3.4	84256	-34762	[illegible]
2007-15	2988255	2619839		0.48	45183	206323	366386	7.5	7.0	6.0	11.0	3.5	94490	-49510	[illegible]
2007-16	3248809	2860932		0.38	39259	223003	387976	7.5	7.0	6.0	11.0	3.5	105185	-65935	[illegible]
2007-17	3521357	3112359		0.26	31468	241083	409938	7.4	7.0	6.0	11.0	3.6	116286	-84820	[illegible]
2007-18	3802438	3373480		0.18	21483	259587	428978	7.4	7.0	6.0	11.0	3.6	127762	-105250	[illegible]

Securitisation: The balance sheets of state governments could also be cleaned through securitisation of past dues. Based on the Ahluwalia (2001) Committee recommendations, a scheme for one-time settlement of outstanding dues of the SEBs to central power sector undertaking (CPSs) by way of securitisation and issuance of power bond to the CPSUs at 8.5 percent tax free bonds has been implemented. Similar schemes could be worked out in terms of over dues on guaranteed bonds/loans contracted earlier to higher costs—where states are constrained to service the repayments.

Statutory limit on size of state's debt/borrowings: In recent times, the issue of fixing limits on overall borrowings of the state governments has come into focus. The EFC had suggested that states cap their debt to 18 percent of their IP/RR. In fact, the overall borrowings of states are construed to a large extent. For example, states are allocated borrowing limits under the market borrowing programme in consultation with the planning Commission; loans from the center are also pre-determined as part of plan assistance; there are limits on WMA and overdraft. However, the special securities issued by NSSF and fund from the public account are not capped. Also the magnitude of funding from such source is by and large beyond the control of state governments. States influence the collections under small savings though aggressive small savings drives and special incentives. In sum, therefore, a hard budget constrain pertes at the state level, The spillover in the revenue deficit of state governments beyond the budgeted figure is accommodated mostly by reduction in capital expenditure. However, means of innovative financing exist through the route of extension of contingent liabilities and guarantees. States, however, are empowered to give guarantees based on some limit, as may be fixed from time to time by the legislature of the state, expended upon the security of the consolidated fund of the state. Thus, an implicit ceiling in state government guarantees is the size of the consolidated fund of the state. It would be better if an explicit cap on the level of states debt is imposed. Respective states could consider placing statutory limit on debt in terms of a ratio of their interest payment to revenue receipts. This would have salutary impact on the risk perception of states borrowings/paper. It would in turn help states access funds at cheaper costs.

Concluding Observations

Given the high level of states outstanding liabilities, certain corrective measures are inevitable. Corrective measures leading to sustainability of debt can be effective only when state government makes a persistent attempt to put their finances on a sound footing by additional revenue effort, expenditure compression and re-prioritization in line with the restructuring plans. The immediate focus of the fiscal reforms should be on achieving revenue balance or, at least, reducing the revenue imbalance to a minimum. Bailouts through write-offs/waivers can never be a long-term solution. Waivers of loans and interest should be strictly restricted so as to void moral hazard problems ad encourage debt repayment discipline. Relief of debt should be incentivised by clearly inking it simple monitorable reforms or process (annexure 8) the process of incentivisation ought to be well thought of so as to fit for all states yet be flexible to adjust for state–specific problems/issues. The monitorable indicators should be uniform, transparent and catch all indicators which can easily be amenable to both expenditure reduction and revenue enhancement.

In fact, it is the controlled component of debt that is focused and monitored and has to an extent been brought down during the 1990s. A drastic reduction in the component of debt which is at market related rates has been observed. It is the uncontrolled segment, the public account borrowings and the off-budged SPV borrowings, which are accessed at higher costs and where the slippages have occurred. A simplistic method of debt restructuring would be to bring down the interest rates on this component in alignment with market rates, however, it is established that debt relief measures alone are no panacea for sustainability of states fiscal situation, unless complimented with appropriate reductions In the primary deficit of the states.

Debt Relief for State Governments Through Finance Commissions

In successive finance commissions, the issue of giving debt relief to the states has bee considered, and has been extended by the following ways; waiving of repayment, reducing interest rates and consolidating of loans. However, the quantum of relief is not very significant as shown I Table 8 below. As pointed out by McCarten, the share of debt relief in the GDP has reduced from 2.95 percent in the Sixth Finance Commission to 0.17 percent in the Eleventh Finance Commission, indicating a decrease in the relative commitment to central debt forgiveness over time. Nonetheless, successive finance commissions have established a tradition of unconditional debt forgiveness.

Table 8: Debt Forgiveness by Finance Commissions

Finance commission	*Year of Report*	*Debt Relief (Rs. crore)*
Sixth	1974	197
Seventh	1979	216
Eight	1984	229
Ninth	1989	98
Tenth	1995	50
Eleventh	2000	340

Upon the Eighth Finance Commission, the statewise allocation of relief was linked to the proportion of the indebtedness of the respective states, relative to the size of their economies. However, the Tenth finance

Commission (TFC) introduced a performance linked debt relief scheme, which was continued by the EFC with certain modifications. The Tenth finance Commission had recommended a scheme of genera debt relief for all states linked to fiscal performance. Improvement of fiscal management was measured by comparing the ratio of revenue receipts (including devolution and grants from the center) to total revenue expenditure in a given year with the average of corresponding ratios in the three immediately preceding years. The performance of each state was measured against its own past performance. Under another scheme proposed by TFC, viz the scheme for encouraging retirement of debt from the proceeds of the disinvestments of equity holdings of state governments, not much headway could be made during the period 1995-00 as only Tamil Nadu could avail of relief of about Rs. 10 crore under this scheme. The EFC discontinued the schemes of debt relief based on disinvestments and fiscal stress and focused only on debt relief linked to improvement in the revenue balance by increasing the extent of potential relief in the fiscal performance linked schemes.

Bibliography

Rao, R. Kavita (2002): Determinants of State-wise Tax Rates in India: A Panel Study mimeo.

Anand, Mukesh, A. Bagchi and T.K. Sen (2001): Fiscal Discipline at the State Level : Preverse Incentives and Paths to Reform, NIPEFP, New Delhi.

Bird, Richard M. (2000): Subnational VATS: Experience and Prospects, mimeo, Rotman School of Management, University of Toronto Canada.

Buiter, W.H. and U.R. Patel (1997); Budgetary Aspects of Stablisation and Structural Adjustment in India: The Painful road to a Sustainbale fiscal Financial Monetary Plan in Blejer M and Ter Minassian (eds.), *Macroeconomic Dimensions of Public Finance,* Routledge, London.

GOI (2000): Report of the Eleventh finance Commission, Government of India; New Delhi.

Settlement of SEB dues, Ministry of Power, New Delhi.

(2002) : The States Fiscal reforms Facility (2000-01 to 2004-05), Ministry of Finance, Government of India, New Delhi.

(2002a): Structuring of APDRP, reform Framework and Principles of financial restructuring of SEBs. Ministry of Power, New Delhi.

(2003a): The fiscal Responsibility and Budget Management Act 2003 (Act No. 39 of 2003), Government of India, New Delhi.

Howes, Stephen and A. Jha (2002): State Finances in India: Towards Fiscal Responsibility. Working paper of the World Bank.

Hughes, Hallett Andrew, P. Minford and A. Rastogi (1993): the European Monetary System : Achievements and Survival in R.C. Bryant, Peter Hooper and C.I. Mann (eds), *Evaluating Policy Regimes, New Research in Empirical Macroeconomics*, Brookings Institution, Washington, Dc.

Joshi, Ravikant (2004): *Value for Money and Municipal Accounting Reforms in Network, India infrastructure Report 2004,* OUP, New Delhi.

Kapur, Devesh and U. Patel (2003): Large Foreign Currency Reserves, *Economic and Political Weekly*, Vol XXXVIII, No. 11, March 15.

McCarten, W.J. (2003): The Challenge of fiscal Discipline in the Indian States in J. Jonathan Rodden, Gunnar Eskeland and Jennie Litvack (eds.), *Fiscal Decentralisation and the Challenge of Hard Budget Constraints*, The World Bank, Washington.

Ma, Jun (1997) Intergovernmental Fiscal Transfer : A Comparison nine counties, Working Paper No. 1822, The World Bank.

Mathur, M.P. (2004) Reforming Property Tax in Patna Municipal Corporation: A Critical analysis in Network. India Infrastructure Report 2004, OUP, New Delhi.

Minford, P. and A. Rastogi (1989): A New Classical policy Programme, in Andrew Britton (ed). *Policy Making with Macroeconomic Models,* Gower Press, England.

Purohit, M.C. (2001): Road Map for National and subnational VARs in India, Discussion paper no. 3. NIPEP, New Delhi.

2002 Harmonising Taxation of Interstate Trade under a Subnational VAT Lesson from International Experience, Discussion paper no.8 NIPFP, New Delhi.

Rao, Govind M (2002) : State Level Fiscal Reforms in India. (www.arts.cornell.edu/econ/indiacon/Rao percent20 papr.pdf)

Rastogi, A.B. (1994) A Rational Expectations Model of the Indian Economy, in H.M. Scobie (ed) *Economic Progress and Growth,* Chapman and Hall, London.

2003: The Infrastructure Sector in India 2001-02 in 3iNetwork. *India Infrastructure Report 2003–Public Expenditure Allocation and Accountability;* OUP, New Delhi.

2003a : State Finances : A Study of Budgets of 2002-03. Reserve Bank of India, Mumbai.

2003b: Annual Report 2002 –03, Reserve Bank of India,Mumbai.

2003c : Report of the Advisory Committee: Ways and Means Advances of State Governments Contents, Reserve Bank of India, Mumbai.

S & P (2003) India (Republic of) (June 30, 2003), Standard and Poors. New York.

Searle, Bob (2002) : Federal Fiscal Relations in Australia – 2001. International Centre for Economic research, Torino, Itlay.

Sen, T.K. (2000) : Reforming State Finances and Intergovernmental Fiscal relations in India. Asian Development Bank, mimeo, paper prepared for ADB, NIPEP.

Vaidya, Chetan and Hitesh Vaidya (2004): Recent fiancial Initiative among Urban Local Bodies : A report in 3 Network, *India infrastructure Report 2004,* OUP, NEW DELHI.

Vaidyanathan, A. (2003): Irrigation Subsidies' in 3iNetwork, India Infrastructure Report 2003 - *Public Expenditure allocation and Accountability,* OUP, New Delhi.

WB 2002 : India–Maharashra Reorienting Government to Facilitate Growth and Reduce poverty, The World Bank.

Ahmad, Ehtisham and Katherine Baer (1997) Colombia in Ter-Minassian Teresa (ed). *Fiscal Federalism in Theory and Practice,* International Monetary Fund, Washington, pp 457-503.

Ahmad, Ehtisham, Bert hofman, Jun Ma, Dick rye, Bob Searle, and Jim Stevenson (1999): Indonesia, Decentralisation – Managing the Risks Aide Memoir to the Minister of Finance, International Monetray Fund, Jakarta (can be accessed on the internet at www.imf.org/external/pubys/ft/seminar/20000/idn/expass.pdf.)

Ahmad, Junaid K. (1998): South Africa: An Intergovernmental Fiscal System in Transition in Bird, Richard M. and François Vaillancourt (eds), *Fiscal Decentralization in Developing Countries,* Cambridge University Press, Cambridge, pp. 239-70.

Alm, James and Jorge Martinez-Vazquez (2002): On the Use of Budgetary Norms as a toll For Fiscal Management. Working Paper #15, International studies Programme, Georgia State University, Atlanta.

Bird, Richard M. and Andrej V. Tarasov (2002): Closing the Gap: fiscal Imbalances and Inter governmental Transfers in Developed Federations, Working Paper #2. International studies programme, Georgia State University, Atlanta.

Bird, Richard M. and Michael Smart (2002). Intergovernmental fiscal Transfers Internation Lessons for Developing countries, World Development pp 899-912.

Bird, Richard M. and Francois Vaillancourt (1998) Fiscal Decentralization in Developing Countries an Overview, in Bird Richard M and Francois Vaillancourt (eds), *Fiscal Decentralization in Developing Countries,* Cambridge University Press, Cambridge, pp. 1-48.

Boex, Jaime (2002): Developing an allocation Formula for the Decentralized Financing and development program, and Implications for the Design of a System of Intergovernmental Fiscal Relations in Nepal, United Nations Capital Development Fund Technical Review Report, Kathmandu, Nepal.

Dafflon, Bernard (1999): Fiscal Federalism in Switzerland: A Survey of Constitional issues, Budget Responsibility and Equalization, Working Paper #278, Department of Political Economy, University of Fribourg, Fribourg.

Dholakia, Ravindra H. (2003): Measurement issues in Comparing Fiscal Performance of States, *Economic and Political Weekly*, March 8, pp. 991-94.

Grewal, Bhajan S. (1999): Federalism and Fiscal Equalisation: Should India Follow the Australian Path, in Ian Copland and John Rickard (eds), *Federalism: Comparative Perspectives from India and Australia*, pp. 249-68, Manohar, New Delhi.

Lalvani, Mala (2002): The Flypaper Effect : Evidence from India, Public Budget ingand Finance, Fall 2002, pp. 67-88.

Martinez-Vazquez, Jorge and Jameson Boex (2002): The design of Equalization Grants: Theory and Application processed, World Bank Institute, The World Bank, Washington, DC.

MeLure, Charles (1997): The Design of inter governmental Grants in Martinex-Vazquez, Jorge, Charles McLure and Sally Wallace, Fiscal Transition in Karakhstan. Asian Development Bank, Manila , pp 317-33.

PWC (2000): Local government Grant Distribution: An International Comparison, Price Warehouse Coopers, London.

Romanik, Clare, Pena Coman, Daniel Daianu and Hernando Garzon (1999) Romania: Winners and Losers: The impact of reform of intergovernmental Transfers, paper prepared for the US Aid Project East European Regional Housing Sector Assistance, Urban Institute, Washington DC.

Shah, Anwar (1998): Indonesia and Pakistan: Fiscal Decentralization: An Elusive Goal in Bird, Richard M. and Francois Vaillancourt (eds) *Fiscal Decentralization in Developing Countries*, Cambridge University Press, Cambridge.

Srivastava, D.K. (2003): India in Yun-hwan, Kim and paul Smoke (eds) *Intergovernmental Fiscal Transfers in Asia: Current Practice and Challenge for the Future*, Asian Development Bank, Manila, pp. 83-137.

Srivastava, D.K. and Tapas K. Sen (2000): Fiscal Federalism in India: Issues Before the Eleventh Finance Commission in Srivastava D.K (Eds), *Fiscal Federalism India*

Contemporary Challenges, pp. 53-86, NIPFP and Har-anand Publications, New Delhi.

Yilmaz, Serdar and Scrap Bindebir (2003): Intergovernmental Transfers concepts and Policy issues, paper prepared for the joint Conference of World Bank Institute and Korea Development Institute on Developing and strengthening the System of Intergovernmental Fiscal Relations and Fiscal decentralisation, Seoul, July 21-23, 2003).

Acharya, S. (2002): India's Macroeconomic Management in the 1990s', *Economic and Political Weekly*, April 20-27, Vol 37 , No.16. pp 1515-38.

Anand, Mukesh, Amaresh Bagchi, Tapas K. Sen (2001) : Fiscal Discipline at the State Level: Perverse Incentives and Paths to reform. Paper presented at NIPFP Seminar on India: Fiscal Publicities to Accelerate Economic Growth, May 21-22.

Blanchard Oliver, Jean-Claude Chouraqui, Robert P. Hagemann and Nichola Sartr (1990): The Sustainability of Fiscal Policy: New Answers to an Old Question, OECD Economic Studies, No. 15, Autumm.

McCarten, W.J. (2001) : The Challenge of Fiscal Discipline in the Indian States, mimeo.

Mohan, R. (2000): Fiscal Correction for Economic Growth : Data Analyze and Suggestions, *Economic and Political Weekly*, June 10-16, vol. 35, No. 24, pp. 2027–36.

Rao, M.G. (2002): State Finances in India: Issues and Challenges, *Economic and Political Weekly*, August 3-9, Vol 37, pp. 3261-71.